May you experience abundant joyous, rollicking laughter.

REJOICE! CLEAN HUMOR

It's good medicine and GREAT exercise!

Your suggestions and comments
about our books will be most welcome!
Please write to the address shown below
or visit one of our websites:

www.UpQuick.com *to order copies of Rejoice! Clean Humor for gift mailing*

www.AV7.org *to find this easy-to-read, accurate literal translation of the Bible*

www.MostEssential.com *to find the Most Essential Truth in the Bible*

www.TrueLoveNeverFails.com *to find the right one for a lasting marriage*

REJOICE! CLEAN HUMOR
Copyright © 2007 by Josef G. Lowder

Published by:
Communication Architects
PO Box 7777
Mesa, Arizona 85216 USA

Library of Congress Control Number 2007907784
Lowder, Josef, 1939-
  Rejoice! Clean Humor : It's good medicine and Great exercise.
  ISBN 0-935597-06-6
  1. American wit and humor. 1. Title.

All rights reserved. No part of this publication may be reproduced in any form without written permission, except for brief excerpts used in reviews in which the source is identified. This compilation includes material accumulated over many years from a wide variety of sources that are believed to be in the public domain and/or are included under the fair-use provision of copyright law.

Printed in the United States of America

Laughing is good exercise. It's like jogging on the inside.

A merry heart does good like a medicine.
But a broken spirit dries up the bones.
Proverbs 17:22

Without a doubt, the very best and most *wholesome, healthy,* and *healing* laughter comes from **clean** humor.

It's great when we can laugh at ourselves and at the very funny things that occur in life ... as long as our laughter is not hurtful, unkind, or offensive to others.

That is the key to clean humor ... to avoid anything that might be degrading or hurtful to anyone. In this book, we feature the very best of hilarious clean humor that steers clear of foul language, mean-spirited ridicule, and any kind of unseemly material.

While collecting, compiling, and editing all these gems, I almost fell out of my chair in convulsions of laughter reading all of the side-splitting anecdotes, one-liners, quips, and quotable quotes. Many of them just seemed to get funnier and funnier each time I re-read them. We hope you will find similar enjoyment in reading and re-reading this book many times and sharing it with others.

Of course, everyones' sense of humor is a little different. You may have heard a few of these gems before, but surely many will be new and will make you laugh out loud again and again, especially when you share them with others.

Rejoice! Clean Humor

While we have tried very hard to stay away from anything that might offend anyone, since we all really do need to be able to laugh at ourselves, we have included a variety of ethnic jokes and a few of those so-called "dumb blonde" jokes.

But please remember, the fictional "dumb blondes" in those jokes are just that, fictional characters. And as every female can explain, those so-called "dumb blonde" jokes are just made that way so they will be simple enough that men can understand them. ☺

All the anecdotes, quips, quotes, and images in this book have been collected over the past 30 years from the public domain. Nothing has been knowingly copied from any other copyrighted published source. However, if you feel that anything included here has not been properly credited or is improper in any way, please tell us and we will certainly make any needed changes in subsequent printings.

Finally, it is important to remember that God Himself certainly does have a great sense of humor. After all, He was the one who created in us the unique human attribute of having a sense of humor and the unique human ability and inclination to smile and laugh.

Several times in the Bible, the Lord's wise counsel is

Be of good cheer!
Matthew 14:27 -&- John 16:33

And *hundreds* of times in the Bible, you will find the word

Rejoice!

Therefore friends ... cheerio ... read on ... Rejoice!
and enjoy a good ***clean*** hearty laugh.

☺

Share some hearty laughter every day!

As you go along your journey through life, you will undoubtedly encounter some BMUPs in the road.

Four things will help you to finish the course well:
- *#1. Choose to have a strong faith in God.*
- *#2. Choose to focus on your God-given purpose.*
- *#3. Choose to maintain a thankful attitude.*
- *#4. Choose to cultivate a great sense of humor.*

✦✦✦ Laughter is _good_ for you! ✦✦✦

Laughter is one of God's greatest gifts to mankind!
Laughter truly is good medicine and GREAT exercise!
Laughter is good for you physically, psychologically, emotionally, intellectually, socially, and even spiritually.

Laughter elevates your mood.
Laughter is evidence of a happy disposition.
Laughter brightens your day . . . and everyone around you.

Laughter is good for your health.
Laughter increases your body's ability to fight disease.
Laughter lowers blood pressure and reduces risk of heart attack.

Laughter also reduces the risk of strokes, ulcers, and arthritis.
Laughter dispels pent-up anxiety, depression, fear, and anger.
Laughter relaxes you, reduces stress, and eases muscle tension.

Laughter improves your brain function.
Laughter enhances your ability and capacity for learning.
Laughter increases your alertness and your attention span.

Laughter increases your productivity.
Laughter improves your creativity in problem solving.
Laughter increases your energy level -- it's a natural pick-me-up.

Laughter is highly contagious . . . _(in a good way)_.
Laughter brings people together.
Laughter unites us and helps us to bond with one another.

Laughter is an amazing universal language.
Laughter breaks down barriers of difference and conflict.
Laughter sounds the same across all languages and cultures.

Laughing and smiling make you more attractive.
Laughter gives you greater confidence in all situations.
Laughter helps to break the ice and improves social interaction.

Laughter can help you communicate more effectively.
Laughter can help you make a better connection with others.
Laughter often succeeds where other methods have failed.

Share some hearty laughter every day!

Laughter makes life fun.
Laughter enhances your peace of mind.
Laughter helps everyone cope with adversity.
Laughter improves your perspective and balance.
Laughter helps you to avoid taking things too seriously.
Laughter replaces negative feelings with positive feelings.
Laughing at our mistakes is better than losing sleep over them.

A hearty laugh gives your body an excellent workout, burning calories, and stimulating almost every system in your body. It has been said that laughter is like jogging on the inside. When you allow yourself to laugh exuberantly, that laughter vigorously exercises your abdominal muscles, your diaphragm, your heart muscles, your respiratory system, your facial, leg, and back muscles. It literally gives you a great massage. It pumps adrenaline into your system and causes more oxygen to flood into your bloodstream.

Laughter improves digestion and intestinal functioning. It strengthens and tones your abdominal muscles. It even changes your brain chemistry, releasing endorphins, the body's natural pain-reducing enzymes, thereby increasing your sense of well-being, improving your reasoning powers, and making you less sensitive to pain and less hampered by it.

Furthermore:
laughter is nonfattening, nonpolluting,
nontaxable, continuously renewable, and FREE.

- ○ Seek out some funny humor each day.
- ○ Laugh more often and more heartily.
- ○ Become a more playful person.
- ○ Surround yourself with humor you enjoy.
- ○ Share some good clean humor with others daily.

Laugh and the world laughs with you.
This book is a great place to begin.

Rejoice! Clean Humor

How to clean a cat

First, thoroughly clean the toilet.

Next, add a cap full of nice pet shampoo to the toilet water.

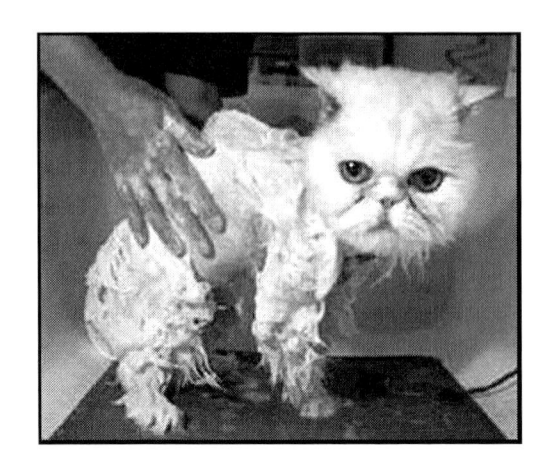

Obtain the cat and soothe him while you carry him to the bathroom.

In one smooth movement, place cat in toilet and quickly close lid.

NOTE: You may need to stand on the toilet lid to keep it closed.

Cat will now self-agitate and make ample suds. Never mind the noises coming from the toilet. Cat is actually enjoying this.

CAUTION: Do not get any part of your body too close to the edge, as cat's claws may be reaching out for anything they can find.

Flush the toilet three or four times. This provides a "powerwash" and "rinse" which I have found to be quite effective.

Have someone open the door to the outside and make sure that there are no people between the toilet and the outside door.

Then stand back as far as you can and lift the lid.

The now-thoroughly clean cat will rocket out of the toilet and streak outside like a bolt of lightning to dry himself.

Sincerely,

The Dog

Share some hearty laughter every day!

✦ Genius Thieves ✦

Some Boeing employees decided to borrow a life raft out of one of the 747s they were working on.

They managed to get the raft out of the plane and into their truck and took it for a float on the river. Moments after they launched the raft, a Coast Guard helicopter arrived on the scene, homing in on the emergency locator beacon that activated when the raft was inflated.

Needless to say, these gentlemen are no longer employed at Boeing.

✦✦✦ Bank Robbery 101 ✦✦✦

A man walked into a downtown bank branch in San Francisco and wrote the following note on a Bank of America deposit slip: "this is a stikkup. put all your muny in this bag." While standing in line, waiting to give the note to the teller, he began to worry that someone might have seen him write the note and might call the police before he got to the teller's window. So, he left the Bank of America and walked across the street to a Wells Fargo branch.

After waiting a few minutes in line there, he handed his note to the Wells Fargo teller. Upon reading it, the teller concluded from the spelling errors that this would-be thief was perhaps not the brightest light in the harbor. So, she told him that she could not accept this stickup note because it was written on a Bank of America deposit slip and that he would either need to fill out a Wells Fargo deposit slip or go back to Bank of America. Looking somewhat defeated, the man said, "OK" and left. A few minutes later, he was arrested while waiting in line back at Bank of America.

Rejoice! Clean Humor

✦✦✦ Backyard Archaeologist ✦✦✦

The following is a transcript of an actual letter sent by the Smithsonian Institute in response to an inquiry

Dear Sir:

Thank you for your latest submission to the Institute, labeled "211-D, layer seven, next to the clothesline post, Hominid skull."

We have given this specimen a careful and detailed examination, and regret to inform you that we disagree with your theory that it represents "conclusive proof of the presence of Early Man in Charleston County two million years ago." Rather, it appears that what you have found is the head of a Barbie doll, of the variety one of our staff, who has small children, believes to be the "Malibu Barbie".

It is evident that you have given a great deal of thought to the analysis of this specimen, and you may be quite certain that those of us who are familiar with your prior work in the field were loathe to come to contradiction with your findings. However, we do feel that there are a number of physical attributes of the specimen which might have tipped you off to it's modern origin:

The material is molded plastic. Ancient hominid remains are typically fossilized bone.

The cranial capacity of the specimen is approximately 9 cubic centimeters, well below the threshold of even the earliest identified proto-hominids.

The dentition pattern evident on the "skull" is more consistent with the common domesticated dog than with the "ravenous man-eating Pliocene clams" that you speculate roamed the wetlands during that time. This latter finding is certainly one of the most intriguing hypotheses you have submitted in your history with this institution, but the evidence seems to weigh rather heavily against it.

Without going into too much detail, let us say that:

Share some hearty laughter every day!

The specimen looks remarkably like the head of a Barbie doll that a dog has chewed on.

Clams don't have teeth.

It is with feelings tinged with melancholy that we must deny your request to have the specimen carbon dated. This is partially due to the heavy load in our lab, and partly due to carbon dating's notorious inaccuracy in fossils of recent geologic record. To the best of our knowledge, no Barbie dolls were produced prior to 1956 AD, and carbon dating is likely to produce wildly inaccurate results.

Sadly, we must also deny your request that we approach the National Science Foundation's Phylogeny Department with the concept of assigning your specimen the scientific name "Australopithecus spiff-arino." Speaking personally, I, for one, fought tenaciously for the acceptance of your proposed taxonomy, but was voted down because the species name you selected was hyphenated, and didn't really sound like it might be Latin. However, we gladly accept your generous donation of this fascinating specimen to the museum.

While it is undoubtedly not a hominid fossil, it is, nonetheless, yet another riveting example of the great body of work you seem to accumulate here so effortlessly. You should know that our Director has reserved a special shelf in his own office for the display of the specimens you have previously submitted to the Institution, and the entire staff speculates daily on what you will happen upon next in your digs at the site you have discovered in your back yard.

We eagerly anticipate your trip to our nation's capital that you proposed in your last letter, and several of us are eager to meet you. We are particularly interested in hearing you expand on your theories surrounding the "trans-positating fillifitation of ferrous ions in a structural matrix" that makes the excellent juvenile Tyrannosaurus Rex femur you recently discovered take on the deceptive appearance of a rusty 9-mm Sears Craftsman automotive crescent wrench.

Yours in Science,
Harvey Rowe, Curator, Antiquities
Paleoanthropology Division, The Smithsonian Institute

✦✦✦ Early warning phone call ✦✦✦

As a senior citizen was driving down the freeway, his car phone rang. Answering, he heard his wife urgently warning him, "Herman, I just heard on the news that there's a car going the wrong way on Interstate 77. Please be careful." Herman replied, "They're all crazy out here, Helen. It's not just one car, it's hundreds of them."

✦✦✦ Beware of tall dark strangers ✦✦✦

In Atlantic City recently, a woman won a bucketful of quarters at a slot machine. So she decided to take a break from the slots to take her winnings up to her room and then go have dinner with her husband. As she carried her coin-filled bucket to the elevator, she was about to step on when she saw two men already aboard. Both were black and one was a very tall, intimidating figure. The woman froze. Her first thought was that these two men were going to rob her, but then her next thought was: "Don't be a bigot. They look like perfectly nice gentlemen." Yet racial stereotypes are powerful and her fear immobilized her. Consequently, she just stood there and stared at the two men, feeling anxious, flustered, and ashamed.

She hoped they didn't read her mind, but then she thought, "Oh surely they must know what I am thinking." Her hesitation about joining them in the elevator was all too obvious now. Her face was flushed. She couldn't just stand there, so with a mighty effort of will she picked up one foot and stepped forward and then followed with the other foot and finally she was on the elevator. Avoiding eye contact, she turned around stiffly and faced the elevator doors as they closed. A second passed, then another second, then another. Her fear increased. The elevator didn't move. Panic consumed her. "Good heavens, she thought, I'm trapped and about to be robbed." Her heart plummeted. Perspiration poured from every pore.

Then one of the men said, "Hit the floor."

Instinct compelled her to immediately do what they told her. The bucket of quarters flew upwards as she threw out her arms and collapsed on the elevator floor. A shower of coins rained down on her. Take my money and spare me, she prayed. More seconds passed.

Share some hearty laughter every day!

Then one of the men politely said, "Ma'am, if you'll just tell us what floor you're going to, we'll push the button." The one who spoke had a little trouble getting the words out while trying mightily to hold in a huge laugh. The woman looked up at the two men as they reached down to help her. Confused, she struggled to her feet.

"When I told my friend here to hit the floor," one said, "I meant that he should hit the elevator button for our floor. I didn't mean for you to hit the floor, ma'am." He spoke genially and bit his lip, very obviously having a hard time trying to keep from laughing.

The woman thought: Oh good grief, what a spectacle I've made of myself. She was too humiliated to speak. She wanted to blurt out an apology, but words failed her. How do you apologize to two perfectly respectable gentlemen for behaving as though they were going to rob you? She didn't know what to say. The three of them gathered up the strewn quarters and refilled her bucket. When the elevator arrived at her floor, they insisted on walking her to her room. She was a little unsteady on her feet now, and they were afraid she might not make it down the corridor.

At her door they bid her a good evening, and as she slipped into her room she could hear them roaring with laughter as they walked back to the elevator. After a few minutes, the woman pulled herself together and went back downstairs for dinner with her husband.

The next morning, a dozen roses were delivered to her room with a crisp one hundred dollar bill attached to each rose. The card read: "Thanks for the best laugh we've had in years."

It was signed: Eddie Murphy & Michael Jordan

✦✦✦ I can hear you just fine ✦✦✦

Three hard of hearing retirees were playing golf one fine March day. One remarked to the other, "Windy, isn't it?" "No," the second man replied, "It's Thursday." Then the third man chimed in, "So am I. Let's go have a drink."

✦✦✦ What red lights? ✦✦✦

Two elderly women were out driving in a large car ... so large that neither could hardly see over the dashboard. As they were cruising along, they came to an intersection. The stoplight was red, but they just sailed right on through without stopping.

The woman in the passenger seat thought to herself "I must be losing it. I could have sworn we just went through a red light."

A bit farther down the road, they approached another intersection and the light was red again. Again, they sailed right through without stopping.

The woman in the passenger seat was almost certain that the light had been red, and she became even more concerned that she was losing it. So she decided to really try to concentrate and pay very close attention at the next intersection.

At the next intersection, sure enough, the light was red and again they sailed right through without stopping.

So this time she turned to her friend and said, "Mildred, did you know that we just went through three red lights in a row? You could have killed us both."

Mildred turned to her friend and said, "Oh, am I driving?"

My memory's not as sharp as it used to be.
Also, my memory's not as sharp as it used to be.

✦✦✦ A perfectly logical explanation ✦✦✦

Officer: "Why were you going so fast?"
Driver: "I was just trying to keep up with the traffic."
Officer: "But there were no other cars around."
Driver: "I know. That's how far ahead of me they are."

Share some hearty laughter every day!

✦✦✦ And you think you had a bad day ✦✦✦

I am writing in response to your request for additional information. In block #3 of the accident report form, I had put "poor planning" as the cause of my accident. In your letter, you said that I should explain further. I trust the following details will be sufficient.

I am a bricklayer by trade. On the day of the accident, I was working alone on the roof of a new six-story building. When I completed my work, I saw that I had about 500 pounds of bricks left. Rather than carry the bricks down by hand I decided to lower them in a barrel by using a pulley that was attached to the building on the sixth floor.

Securing the rope at the ground level, I went up to the roof and loaded the bricks into the barrel. I then went back to the ground, untied the rope, and held it tightly to ensure a slow descent of the 500 pounds of bricks. You will note in block #11 of the accident report form that I weigh 135 pounds. Due to my surprise at being jerked off the ground so suddenly, I forgot to let go of the rope. Needless to say, I proceeded rapidly up the side of the building. In the vicinity of the third floor, I met the barrel coming down. This explains the fractured scull and broken collarbone. Slowed only slightly, I continued my rapid ascent, not stopping until the fingers of my right hand were jammed two knuckles deep into the pulley. Fortunately, by this time I had regained my presence of mind and was able to hold tightly to the rope, in spite of my pain.

At approximately the same time, the barrel of bricks hit the ground and the bottom fell out of the barrel. Emptied of the weight of the bricks, the barrel now weighed approximately 50 pounds. I refer you again to my weight in block #11. Thus I now began a rapid descent back down the side of the building.

In the vicinity of the third floor, I met the barrel coming up. This accounts for my fractured ankles and lacerations. The encounter with the barrel, slowed me enough to lessen my injuries when I fell onto the pile of bricks and fortunately, only three vertebrae were cracked. I am sorry to report, however, that as I lay there on the bricks in pain, unable to move, and watching the barrel six stories above, I again lost my presence of mind ... and let go of the rope.

Rejoice! Clean Humor

✦ Some bumper stickers make a good point ✦

> Cover me, I'm changing lanes.

Everyone has a photographic memory.
Some just don't have any film.

> I used to have a handle on life, but it broke off.

Try not to let your mind wander.
It is too small and fragile to be out by itself.

> Welcome to America. Now speak English.

I refuse to have a battle of wits
with an unarmed person.

> Caution: Driver legally blonde.

How many roads must a man travel down
before he admits he is lost?

> If we quit voting will they all go away?

All men are animals.
Some just make better pets.

> Eat right, exercise, die anyway.

Some minds are like concrete
thoroughly mixed up and permanently set.

> Body by Nautilus, Brain by Mattel.

Therapy is expensive.
Popping bubble wrap is cheap.
You choose.

> Illiterate? Write for help.

Share some hearty laughter every day!

This day was a total waste of makeup.

Make yourself at home.
Clean my kitchen.

Does your train of thought have a caboose?

Who are these kids
and why are they calling me Mom?

See no evil, hear no evil, date no evil.

I started out with nothing
and I still have most of it left.

Allow me to introduce myselves.

Just whisper my favorite words:
"I'll buy it for you."

Better living through denial.

Stress is when you wake up screaming
and realize you haven't fallen asleep yet.

Adults are just kids who owe money.

Nice perfume.
Must you marinate in it?

Ambivalent? Well, yes and no.

I'm not tense,
just terribly, terribly alert.

He who laughs last just didn't get it.

Always remember you are unique …
… just like everybody else.

Rejoice! Clean Humor

✦ Hilarious quotes from the rich and famous ✦ athletes, celebrities, officials, and more

From the Department of Social Services, Greenville, South Carolina
"Your food stamps will be stopped effective March 1992 because we received notice that you passed away. May God bless you. You may reapply if there is a change in your circumstances."

"Outside of the killings, Washington D.C. has one of the lowest crime rates in the country." --Marion Barry, as Mayor of D.C.

"We've got to pause and ask ourselves: How much clean air do we need?" --Former Chrysler Chairman Lee Iacocca

"My advice is, get married. If you find a good wife you'll be happy. If not, you'll become a philosopher. --Socrates

"We don't necessarily discriminate. We simply exclude certain types of people." --ROTC Instructor Colonel Gerald Wellman

"Half this game is ninety percent mental."
--Philadelphia Phillies Manager Danny Ozark

University of Pittsburgh senior basketball player: "I'm going to graduate on time, no matter how long it takes."

University of Houston receiver Torrin Polk on his coach, John Jenkins: "He treats us like men. He lets us wear earrings."

University of Kentucky basketball forward Winston Bennett: "I've never had major knee surgery on any other part of my body."

North Carolina State basketball player Chuck Nevitt, explaining why he appeared nervous at practice: "My sister is expecting a baby and I don't know if I'm going to be an uncle or an aunt."

Utah Jazz president Frank Layden on a former player: "I asked him, 'Son, what is it with you? Is it ignorance or apathy?' He said, "Coach, I don't know and I don't care."

Share some hearty laughter every day!

Baseball announcer: "If history repeats itself, I should think we can expect the same thing again."

Basketball commentator: "He dribbles a lot and the opposition doesn't like it. In fact you can see it all over their faces."

Boxing commentator: "Sure there have been injuries and even some deaths in boxing, but none of them really that serious."

Football commentator and former pro quarterback Joe Theismann: "Nobody in football should be called a genius. A genius is a guy like Norman Einstein."

"The reason the all-American boy prefers beauty over brains is that the all-American boy can see better than he can think." -- Farrah Fawcett Majors

Movie producer Samual Goldwyn: "A verbal contract isn't worth the paper it's written on."

I was married by a judge. I should have asked for a jury. --Groucho Marx

Sometimes, when I look at my children, I say to myself: "Lillian, you should have remained a virgin." --Lillian Carter

"Smoking kills, and if you're killed, you've lost a very important part of your life." --Brooke Shields, during an interview to become spokesperson for a federal anti-smoking campaign.

Motivational writer and speaker Zig Ziglar:
"People often say that motivation doesn't last.
Well, neither does bathing.
That's why we recommend it daily."

> *A simple way to take the measure of a country is to look at how many want in ... and how many want out.* --Tony Blair

Rejoice! Clean Humor

✦ Impressive Funeral ✦

John's will provided $30,000 for an elaborate funeral.

As the last guests departed from the affair, his wife Mary turned to her friend and said: "Well, I'm sure John would be pleased."

"I'm sure you're right," her friend Jane said, as she lowered her voice and leaned in close. "How much did this affair really cost?"

"I spent all thirty-thousand," Mary replied. "No, really?" Jane exclaimed. "I mean, it was very nice, but $30,000?"

Mary explained: "Well, the funeral was $6,500. I donated $500 to the church. The wake, food, and drinks were another $500. And the rest went for the memorial stone."

Jane quickly computed the difference and said, "My goodness, Mary, $22,500 for a memorial stone? How big is it?"

Mary replied: "Two and a half carats."

Making a big fuss over doctrinal distinctives is foolishness, and labels are really meaningless, because they either blow off as you're going up or burn off as you're going down.

✦✦✦ Chinese Proverbs ✦✦✦

- Man who run in front of car get tired.
- Man who run behind car get exhausted.
- Man who drive like hell, bound to get there.
- Man who eat many prunes get good run for money.
- War not determine who is right, war determine who is left.

Share some hearty laughter every day!

✦✦✦ The AAADD Syndrome ✦✦✦

Someone recently diagnosed with AAADD (Age Activated Attention Deficiency Disorder) explained the symptoms this way:

I decided to wash my car. As I started toward the garage, I noticed that there was mail on the hall table. So, I decided to go through the mail before I washed the car. I laid my car keys on the table, put the junk mail in the trash can under the table, and noticed that the trash can was full. So, I decided to put the bills back on the table and take out the trash first.

But then I thought, since I'm going to be near the mailbox when I take out the trash anyway, I may as well pay the bills first. So, I took my checkbook out of my briefcase that was on the table and noticed that there was only one check left. My extra checks were in my desk in the den, so I went back to my desk where I noticed a bottle of soda that I had been drinking.

I was going to look for my checks, but first I needed to push the soda aside so I wouldn't accidentally knock it over. In doing that, I noticed that the soda was getting warm and decided I should put it in the refrigerator to keep it cold.

As I headed toward the kitchen with the soda, a vase of flowers on the counter caught my eye. They needed to be watered, so, I sat the soda down on the counter and then I saw my reading glasses that I had been searching for all morning. I decided that I had better put them back on my desk ... but then I remembered that I was going to water the flowers. So, I put the glasses back down on the counter, filled a container with water ... and suddenly I spotted the TV remote. Someone had left it on the kitchen table.

No doubt tonight when we go to watch TV, we will be looking for the remote, but nobody will remember that it was on the kitchen table, so I decided to put it back in the den where it belongs. But first, I'll water the flowers. I splashed some water on the flowers, but most of it spilled on the floor. So, I put the remote back down on the table, got some towels to wipe up the spill and then I headed down the hall, trying to remember what I had been planning to do.

Rejoice! Clean Humor

At the end of the day: the car isn't washed, the bills aren't paid, there is a warm bottle of soda sitting on the counter, the flowers aren't watered, there is still only one check in my checkbook, I can't find the remote, can't find my glasses, and don't remember what I did with the car keys.

Then when I try to figure out why nothing got done today, I'm really baffled because I know I was busy all day long, and I'm really tired.

✦✦✦ Interview Slam Sunk ✦✦✦

An executive was interviewing a young blonde for a position in his company. He wanted to find out something about her personality so he asked, "If you could have a conversation with someone living or dead, who would it be?" Without hesitating, the blonde replied, "The living one."

✦✦✦ Accident Claim Explanations ✦✦✦

Believe it or not, these are actual accident claim explanations and descriptions as they were written on insurance claim forms:

- I started to slow down but the traffic was more stationary than I thought.

- I moved from the center lane to the fast lane but the other car didn't give way.

- I didn't think the speed limit applied after midnight.

- The car in front hit the pedestrian but he got up, so I hit him again.

- I had been driving for 40 years when I fell asleep at the wheel and had an accident.

- Coming home, I drove into the wrong house and collided with a tree I don't have.

Share some hearty laughter every day!

- The other car collided with mine without giving any warning of its intentions.

- I thought my window was down, but found it wasn't when I put my head through it.

- I collided with a stationary truck coming the other way.

- In an attempt to kill a fly, I drove into a telephone pole.

- I had been shopping all day and was on my way home when a hedge sprang up and obscured my vision so I did not see the other car.

- I was on my way to the doctor with rear end trouble when my universal joint gave way causing me to have an accident.

- To avoid hitting the bumper of the car in front, I struck the pedestrian.

- I was thrown from the car as it left the road and was found later in a ditch by some stray cows.

- An invisible car came out of nowhere, struck my car, and then vanished.

- The pedestrian had no idea which way to run, so I ran over him.

- I saw a slow-moving, sad faced old gentleman, as he bounced off the roof of my car.

- A pedestrian hit me and went under my car.

- The guy was all over the road. I had to swerve a number of times before I hit him.

- The indirect cause of the accident was a little guy in a small car with a big mouth.

Isn't it amazing how it is always the other guy's fault?

Rejoice! Clean Humor

> *Many years ago in Scotland*
> *a game was invented and given the title:*
> *"Gentlemen Only ... Ladies Forbidden"*
>
> *Thus the game came to be known as ... GOLF*

✦ Some golfers are remarkably thoughtful ✦

A man and his friend were playing golf at their local golf course, and as he was about to chip onto the green, he looked up and noticed a long funeral procession on the road next to the course. So, he stopped in mid-swing, took off his golf cap, closed his eyes, and bowed his head in prayer.

His friend said, "Wow, that is the most thoughtful and touching thing I have ever seen. You truly are a kind man."

The man replied, "Yes, well, we were married for 35 years."

✦✦✦ Airline Maintenance Solutions ✦✦✦

After every flight, pilots fill out a form called a gripe sheet that tells the aircraft mechanics about any problems or potential problems encountered with the aircraft during their last flight. The mechanics investigate and correct these problems and respond in writing on the lower half of the form to describe what corrective actions have been taken. Pilots then review this gripe sheets and the corrections made before their next flight.

Never let it be said that ground crews and engineers lack a sense of humor. Following are some actual logged problem reports submitted by Quantas pilots and the report of solutions applied by maintenance engineers. *(It is worthy of note that at the time this was prepared, Quantas was the only major airline that had never had an accident ... so, they must have been doing something right.)*

Share some hearty laughter every day!

Problem: Left inside main tire almost needs replacement.
Solution: Almost replaced left inside main tire.

Problem: Something loose in cockpit.
Solution: Something tightened in cockpit.

Problem: Dead bugs on windshield.
Solution: Live bugs on back-order.

Problem: Evidence of leak on right main landing gear.
Solution: Evidence removed.

Problem: DME volume unbelievably loud.
Solution: DME volume set to more believable level.

Problem: Friction locks cause throttle levers to stick.
Solution: That is what they're for.

Problem: IFF inoperative.
Solution: IFF always inoperative in OFF mode.

Problem: Suspected crack in windshield.
Solution: Suspect you're right.

Problem: Number 3 engine missing.
Solution: After a brief search, engine found on right wing.

Problem: Aircraft handles funny.
Solution: Aircraft warned to straighten up, fly right, and be serious.

Problem: Target radar hums.
Solution: Reprogrammed target radar with lyrics.

Problem: Noise coming from under instrument panel.
   Sounds like a midget pounding on something with a hammer.
Solution: Took hammer away from midget.

*Genius may have its limitations,
but stupidity is not thus handicapped.*

Rejoice! Clean Humor

✦✦✦ Airline Cabin Announcements ✦✦✦

to make in-flight announcements a bit more entertaining

- Welcome aboard Southwest. To operate your seat belt, insert the metal tab into the buckle and pull tight. It works just like every other seat belt; and, if you don't know how to operate one, you probably shouldn't be out in public unsupervised.

- Should the cabin lose pressure, oxygen masks will drop from the overhead area. Place the mask over your own nose and mouth before assisting children ... or other adults who are acting like children.

- In the event of an emergency water landing, your seat cushions can be used for flotation. So please paddle to shore and feel free to take them with you with our compliments.

- On a flight with a very senior flight attendant crew, the pilot said, "Ladies and gentlemen, we've reached cruising altitude and will be turning down the cabin lights for your comfort and to enhance the appearance of your flight attendants."

- Weather at our destination is 50 degrees with some broken clouds, but we'll try to have them fixed before we arrive. Thank you for flying with us and remember, nobody loves you ... or your money ... more than Southwest Airlines.

- As the plane landed and was coming to a stop, a voice came over the loudspeaker: "Whoa, big fella. WHOA!"

- After a rough landing during thunderstorms in Memphis, a flight attendant on a Northwest flight announced, "Please take care when opening the overhead compartments because, after a landing like that, you can be sure everything has shifted."

- After another less than perfect landing, an attendant said: "Please remain seated as Captain Kangaroo bounces us to the terminal."

- Thank you for flying Delta. We hope you enjoyed giving us the business as much as we enjoyed taking you for a ride.

Share some hearty laughter every day!

- On a Southwest flight after a very hard landing, the attendant came on the intercom and said, "That was quite a bump and I know what y'all are thinking; but I am here to tell you that this was not the pilot's fault, it was not our flight attendant's fault, and it was not our airline's fault. It was the asphalt's fault."

- On a very windy day, during the final approach, the captain was really having to fight it. So then after an extremely hard landing, the flight attendant said, "Ladies and Gentlemen, please remain in your seats with your seat belts securely fastened while the captain taxis what's left of our airplane to the gate."

- Upon arriving at their destination, another flight attendant made the following announcement: "We'd like to thank you folks for flying with us today, and the next time you get the insane urge to go blasting through the skies in a pressurized metal tube, we hope you'll think of US Airways."

- As you exit the plane, make sure to gather all of your belongings. Anything left behind will be distributed evenly among the flight attendants. Please do not leave children or spouses.

- One airline had a policy that required the pilot to stand at the door while the passengers exited, greet them and tell them thanks for flying XYZ airline. After a very hard landing, the pilot was having a difficult time looking passengers in the eye, as he anticipated some smart comments.

  After everyone had gotten off except for one little old lady walking with a cane, she came up to him and said, "Sonny, mind if I ask you a question?" The pilot said, "Why no, ma'am." The little old lady said, "Did we land or were we shot down?"

- After a real crusher of a landing in Phoenix, the flight attendant came on with, "Ladies and Gentlemen, please remain in your seats until Captain Crash and the Crew have brought the aircraft to a screeching halt against the gate. And, once the tire smoke has cleared and the warning bells are silenced, we'll open the door and you can pick your way through the wreckage to the terminal."

Rejoice! Clean Humor

✦✦✦ Just send in the Marines ✦✦✦

As an atheist professor was teaching a college class, he told the class that he was going to prove that there is no God.

So he said, "God, if you really exist, then I want you to knock me off this platform. I'll give you 15 minutes."

Ten minutes went by and he kept taunting God, saying, "Here I am, God. I'm still waiting." He continued for several minutes ...

... then a big, muscular Marine just released from active duty and newly registered in the class walked up to the professor and smacked him full force in the face, sending him flying from the platform.

The professor struggled to his feet, obviously shaken, and yelled,

"What's the matter with you? Why did you do that?"

The Marine said, "God was busy. He sent me."

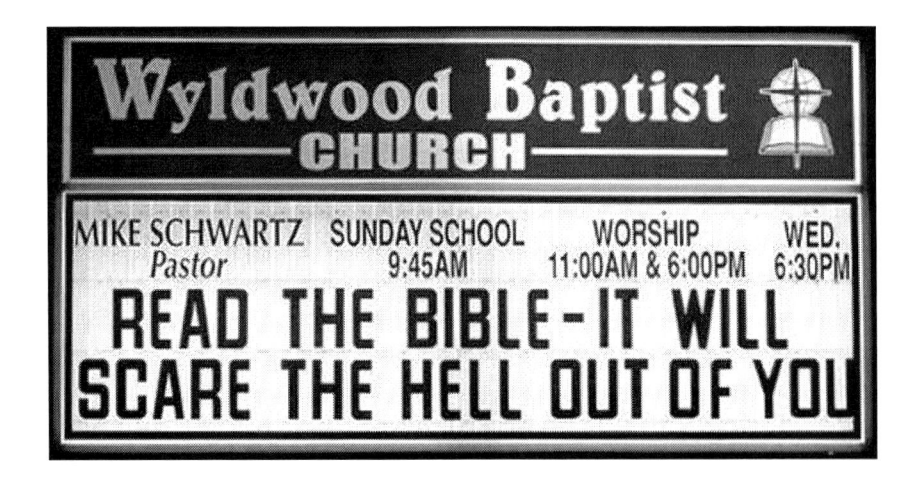

Wyldwood Baptist CHURCH

MIKE SCHWARTZ SUNDAY SCHOOL WORSHIP WED.
Pastor 9:45AM 11:00AM & 6:00PM 6:30PM

READ THE BIBLE - IT WILL SCARE THE HELL OUT OF YOU

✦ Here's the logic of the theory of evolution: ✦

If a million monkeys typed on a million keyboards for a million years, eventually all the works of Shakespeare would be produced.

Share some hearty laughter every day!

✦✦ The Art of Direct and Cross Examination ✦✦
by learned counsel

Attorney: Now, doctor, isn't it true that when a person dies in his sleep, in most cases he just passes quietly away and doesn't know anything about it until the next morning?

Attorney: What happened then?
Witness: He said, "I have to kill you because you can identify me."
Attorney: Did he kill you?

Attorney: Your youngest son, the 20-year-old, how old is he?

Attorney: Were you alone or by yourself?

Attorney: How long have you been a French Canadian?

Attorney: Do you have any children or anything of that kind?

Attorney: I now show you exhibit 3. Do you recognize this picture.
Witness: That's me.
Attorney: Were you present when that picture was taken?

Attorney: Mrs. Johnson, how was your first marriage terminated?
Witness: By death.
Attorney: And by whose death was it terminated?

Attorney: Do you know how far pregnant you are now?
Witness: It will be three months on November 8.
Attorney: So apparently the date of conception was August 8?
Witness: Yes.
Attorney: What were you doing at that time?

Attorney: Were you present in court room this morning when you were sworn in?

Attorney: You say that the stairs went down to the basement?
Witness: Yes.
Attorney: And these stairs, did they also go up?

Rejoice! Clean Humor

Attorney: She had three children, right?
Witness: Yes.
Attorney: How many were boys?
Witness: None.
Attorney: Were there girls?

An attorney, realizing he was on the verge of unleashing a stupid question, interrupted himself and said, "Your Honor, I'd like to strike the next question."

Attorney: Do you recall approximately the time that you examined the body of Mr. Williamson at the rose Chapel?
Witness: It was in the evening. The autopsy started about 8:30 p.m.
Attorney: Mr. Williamson was dead at the time, is that correct?
Witness: No, you ding-a-ling. He was sitting up on the table and wondering why I was doing an autopsy.

Attorney: What is your brother-in-law's name?
Witness: Vorokin.
Attorney: What's his first name?
Witness: I can't remember.
Attorney: He's been your brother-in-law for years and you can't remember his name?
Witness: No. I tell you I'm too excited *(rising from witness chair)*. For goodness sake, Nathan, tell him your name.

Attorney: Did you ever stay all night with this man in New York?
Witness: I refuse to answer that question.
Attorney: Did you ever stay all night with this man in Chicago?
Witness: I refuse to answer that question.
Attorney: Did you ever stay all night with this man in Miami?
Witness: No.

Attorney: Doctor, did you say he was shot in the woods?
Witness: No, I said he was shot in the lumbar region.

Attorney: What is your name?
Witness: Mary Ann Jones.
Attorney: And what is your marital status?
Witness: Fair.

Share some hearty laughter every day!

Attorney: Are you married?
Witness: No, I'm divorced.
Attorney: And what did your husband do before you divorced him?
Witness: A lot of things I didn't know about.

Attorney: How did you happen to go to Dr. Smith?
Witness: Well, a gal down the road had had several of her children by him, and she said he was really good.

Attorney: Do you believe you are emotionally unstable?
Witness: I should be.
Attorney: And how many times have you committed suicide?
Witness: Four times.

Attorney: Doctor, how many autopsies have you performed on dead people?
Witness: All my autopsies have been on dead people.

Attorney: Were you acquainted with the deceased?
Witness: Yes.
Attorney: Before or after he died?

Attorney: Officer, what led you to believe this man was under the influence?
Witness: Because he was argumentinary and couldn't pronunciate his words.

Attorney: Mrs. Jones, is your appearance here this morning pursuant to a deposition notice I sent to your attorney?
Witness: No. This is how I dress when I go to work.

Attorney: Now, as we begin, I must ask you to banish all present information and prejudice from your minds, if you have any.

Attorney: Did he pick up the dog by his ears?
Witness: No.
Attorney: What was he doing with the dog's ears?
Witness: Picking them up in the air?
Attorney: Where was the dog at this time?
Witness: Attached to the ears.

Rejoice! Clean Humor

Attorney to a grade school student: Gary, all of your answers must be oral, okay? Now, what school did you go to?
Witness: Oral.

Attorney: What is your relationship with the plaintiff?
Witness: She is my daughter.
Attorney: And was she your daughter on February 13, 1979?

Attorney: Now you have investigated other murders, have you not, where there was a victim?

Attorney: And what did he do then?
Witness: He came home, and the next morning he was dead.
Attorney: So when he woke up the next morning he was dead?

Attorney: Did you tell your lawyer that your husband had offered you indignities?
Witness: He didn't offer me nothing but the furniture.

Attorney: Are you qualified to give a urine sample?
Witness: Yes, I have been since early childhood.

Attorney: Were you shot in the fracas?
Witness: No. I was shot halfway between the fracas and the naval.

Attorney: *(showing a picture)* That's you?
Witness: Yes.
Attorney: Were you present when the picture was taken?

Attorney: Could you see him from where you were standing?
Witness: I could see his head.
Attorney: And where was his head?
Witness: Just above his shoulders.

Prosecuting Attorney: When he went, had you gone and had she, if she wanted to and was able, for the time being excluding all restraints on her not to go, gone also, would he have brought you, meaning you and she, with him to the station?
Defense Attorney: Objection. That question should be taken out and shot.

Share some hearty laughter every day!

✦✦✦ Baptismal service down by the river ✦✦✦

One Sunday afternoon, an inebriated gentleman came stumbling upon a baptismal service down by the river and he proceeded to walk down into the water and stood next to the preacher. The preacher said to him: "Well, mister, are you ready to find Jesus?"

The drunk looked back at him a bit blurry eyed and with a slurred speech, he said: "Yes-suh, preacher, I shore am."

So, the minister lowered the drunk down into the water and quickly pulled him back up saying: "Have you found Jesus, brother?"

The drunk said: "Nooooo-suh, I shore ain't."

So, the preacher dunked him again, for a bit longer this time, and then brought him back up and said: "Well have you found Jesus now, brother?"

The drunk sputtered and said: "Nooooo, I have not, reverend."

So, the preacher, who was beginning to be a bit disgusted now, dunked the old drunk back down in the river a third time and held him there for about 30-seconds. When he brought him back up this time, in a rather harsh tone, he said: "My God, man, have you found Jesus yet?"

The old drunk coughed and sputtered and wiped his eyes and said:

"Nooooo, I have not. Are you sure this is where he fell in?"

✦✦ Eloquent prayer ... prompts a question ✦✦

A visiting minister was eloquent during the offertory prayer. "Dear Lord," he began, with arms extended toward heaven and a rapturous look on his upturned face, "Without you we are but dust ..."

At that very solemn instant, an attentive little girl leaned over to her mother and in a sweet but very loud little voice asked: "Mommy, what is butt dust?"

Rejoice! Clean Humor

✦✦✦ Born a Baptist ... but now? ✦✦✦

Every Friday night, Bubba fired up his outdoor grill and cooked a venison steak. Now Bubba's neighbors were all Catholics and were forbidden from eating meat on Friday, so the delicious aroma of grilled venison was causing quite a problem for them.

So, they went to their priest to ask if perhaps he might be able to do something about this. Well, the priest went to Bubba's house for a visit and suggested that he become a Catholic. Bubba consented.

After several classes and much study, Bubba attended his first Mass. As the priest sprinkled holy water over him, he said, "You were born a Baptist and raised a Baptist, but now you are a Catholic."

Bubba's neighbors were greatly relieved about Bubba's conversion ... that is until the very next Friday night when that wonderful aroma of grilled venison filled the air once again.

So the neighbors called the priest again to report this matter and the priest immediately rushed to Bubba's house, clutching a rosary and preparing to scold him. But he stopped in his tracks and watched in amazement as he observe Bubba standing over the barbeque grill with a small bottle of holy water that he was carefully sprinkling over the grilling meat and ... and solemnly chanting:

> "You wuz born a deer and you wuz raised a deer,
> but now you is a catfish."

And going to church doesn't make you a Christian any more than standing in a garage makes you a car.

Share some hearty laughter every day!

✦✦✦ The Middle Wife ✦✦✦
as told by a second grader

Show-and-tell is usually a pretty tame event as kids bring in pet turtles, model airplanes, pictures of fish they've caught, and other innocent things like that. But one day, a bright, outgoing little girl named Erica came to the front of the class with a pillow stuffed under her sweater, held up a snapshot of an infant, and said: "This is my baby brother, and I am going to tell you about his birthday."

"Mom and Dad made him as a symbol of their love. Dad put a seed in my Mom's stomach and Luke grew in there. He ate for nine months through an umbrella cord."

All the kids watched in amazement as little Erica stood there with her hands on the pillow and continued her show and tell story.

"Two Saturdays ago, my Mom started saying, 'Oh, oh, oh'." Erica put a hand behind her back and groaned as she walked around the room. "Mom walked around for an hour, saying 'Oh, oh, oh'." Erica was now doing an absolutely hysterical duck walk, holding her back and groaning as she continued her story:

"So, my Dad called the middle wife ... she delivers babies ... but she didn't have a sign on her car like the Domino's man. They all got my Mom to lie down in bed like this." Now Erica simulated laying down with her back against the wall.

"And then all of a sudden, pop! My Mom had this big bag of water that she kept in there in case the baby got thirsty, and it just blew up and spilled all over the bed ... like psshhheew."

Now, Erica had her legs spread and her little hands are miming water flowing away. Absolutely hysterical!

"And then the middle wife started saying, 'Push, push, and breathe, breathe' ... and they all started counting. But they never even got past ten when all of a sudden, out came my brother. He was all covered in yucky stuff, which they said was from Mom's play-center. So, I guess there sure must be a lot of stuff inside there."

Rejoice! Clean Humor

✧ Trying to grade papers with a straight face ✧

The following are actual answers to a parochial elementary school test about the Old and New Testaments as written by the children. Watch the word choices and spellings closely to get the full effect.

1. In the first book of the Bible, Guinessis, God got tired of creating the world, so He took the Sabbath as a day off.

2. Adam and Eve were created from an apple tree. Noah's wife was Joan of Ark, and the animals came on Noah's Ark in pears.

3. Lots wife was a pillar of salt during the day, but a ball of fire during the night.

4. The Jews were a proud people and throughout history they had trouble with unsympathetic genitals.

5. Sampson was a strong man who let himself be led astray by a jezebel like Delilah.

6. Sampson slayed the Philistines with the axe of the apostles.

7. Moses led the Jews to the Red Sea where they made unleaven bread which is bread without any ingredients.

8. The Egyptians were all drowned in the dessert. Afterwards, Moses went up to Mount Cyanide to get the Ten Commandments.

9. The first commandment was when Eve commanded Adam to eat the apple.

10. The seventh commandment is thou shalt not admit adultery.

11. Moses died before he ever reached Canada. Then Joshua led the Hebrews in the battle of geritol.

12. The greatest miricle in the Bible is when Joshua told his son to stand stil and he obeyed him.

Share some hearty laughter every day!

13. David was a Hebrew king who was skilled at playing the liar. He fought with the Finkelsteins, a race of people who lived in biblical times.

14. Solomon had 300 wives and 700 porcupines.

15. When Mary heard she was the mother of Jesus, she sang the Magna Carta.

16. When the three wise guys from the east side arrived they found Jesus in the manager.

17. Jesus was born because Mary had an immaculate contraption.

18. St. John the blacksmith dumped water on Jesus' head.

19. Jesus enunciated the golden rule which says to do unto others before they do one to you. He also explained that a man doth not live by sweat alone.

20. It was a miricle when Jesus rose from the dead and managed to get that huge tombstone off the entrance.

21. The people who followed the Lord were called the 12 decibels.

22. The epistels were the wives of the apostles.

23. One of the opposums was St. Matthew who was also a taximan.

24. St. Paul cavorted to Christianity and than he preached holy acrimony, which is another name for marriage.

25. Christians have only one spouse. This is called monotony.

---

*God loves everyone,
but He prefers "fruits of the spirit"
over "religious nuts."*

✢✢✢ **Daffynitions** ✢✢✢

Acupuncture: A jab well done.
Arbitrator: A cook that leaves Arby's to work at McDonald's
Avoidable: What a bullfighter tries to do
Baloney: Where some hemlines fall
Bernadette: The act of torching a mortgage
Burglarize: What a crook sees with
Counterfeiters: Workers who put together kitchen cabinets
Eclipse: What an English barber does for a living
Eyedropper: A clumsy ophthalmologist
Heroes: What a guy in a boat does
Hipatitis: Terminal coolness.
Left Bank: What the robber did when his bag was full of loot
Misty: How golfers create divots
Paradox: Two physicians
Parasites: What you see from the top of the Eiffel Tower
Pharmacist: A helper on the farm
Polarize: What penguins see with
Primate: Removing your spouse from in front of the TV
Relief: What trees do in the spring
Rubberneck: What you do to relax your wife
Seamstress: When someone wears clothes too small
Selfish: What the owner of a seafood store does
Subdued: A guy who works on one of those submarines, man
Sudafed: Bringing litigation against a government official
A will: A dead giveaway.

Sarcasm:
The gap between
something written with a sarcastic wit
and the person who doesn't get it.

Share some hearty laughter every day!

✦✦✦ Very Punny ✦✦✦

- Atheism is a non-prophet religion.
- A bicycle can't stand alone because it is two-tired.
- A chicken crossing the road is poultry in motion.
- If you don't pay your exorcist you will get repossessed.
- Show me a piano falling down a mine shaft and I'll show you A-flat minor.
- When a clock is hungry it goes back four seconds.
- The man who fell into an upholstery machine is fully recovered.
- A grenade thrown into a kitchen in France would result in Linoleum Blownapart.
- You feel stuck with your debt if you can't budge it.
- A boiled egg in the morning is hard to beat.
- The short fortune teller who escaped from prison was a small medium at large.
- Those who get too big for their britches will be exposed in the end.
- When you've seen one shopping center you've seen a mall.
- When the actress saw her first strands of gray hair she thought she would dye.
- Bakers trade bread recipes on a knead to know basis.
- Santa's helpers are subordinate clauses.
- Marathon runners with bad footwear suffer the agony of defeat.
- I wondered why the baseball was getting bigger. Then it hit me.
- Police were called to a daycare center where a three-year-old was resisting a rest.
- To try to write with a broken pencil is pointless.
- The child didn't admit that he ate some glue. His lips were sealed.

Rejoice! Clean Humor

✦✦✦ "Dumb" ... like a fox ✦✦✦

A gorgeous blonde in a classy business suit walked into a large bank in downtown Los Angeles and asked to borrow $5,000 for a two-week business trip.

When the loan officer asked for some collateral, the blonde tossed him the keys to her new Mercedes. The bank officer chuckled inside himself at the apparent "dumbness" of this blonde using a $100,000 car as collateral for a $5,000 loan, but he approved the loan, took the keys, and drove the car to the bank's secure garage.

Two weeks later, the blonde came back into the bank and repaid the loan plus the accrued interest of $15.

"Thanks for your business," the loan officer said with a sly smirk.

"Thanks for keeping my car safe for two weeks," the savvy blonde replied with a wink. "You certainly do have the cheapest parking garage in this city."

> *Never let it be said that all blondes are "dumb!"*
> *The following so-called "dumb blonde" jokes*
> *are just a way of poking fun at ourselves -- all of us!*

Two blondes were working on a house. As one was nailing on siding, she would reach into her nail pouch, pull out a nail, and either toss it over her shoulder or nail it in. The other blonde said, "What are you doing? Why are you throwing those nails away?"

The first blonde explained, "Well, some of the nails I pull out of the pouch are pointed toward me, so I throw those away because they are defective. But when a nail is pointed toward the house, then I know it is okay so I nail it in."

The second blonde was quite irked about wasting all those nails, and she said, "You ding-a-ling, those nails pointed toward you are not defective! They're for the other side of the house!"

Share some hearty laughter every day!

✦✦✦ She was sooooo blonde ✦✦✦

- She thought a quarterback was a refund.
- She thought General Motors was in the army.
- She thought Meow Mix was a CD for cats.
- She thought Boyz II Men was a day care center.
- At the bottom of an application where it says "Sign here:" she wrote "Sagittarius."

She was sooooo blonde ...
- She took the ruler to bed to see how long she slept.
- She sent a fax with a stamp on it.
- Under "education" on her job application, she put "Hooked On Phonics."

She was sooooo blonde ...
- She tripped over a cordless phone.
- She spent 20 minutes looking at the orange juice can ... because it said Concentrate."
- She told her friend to meet her at the corner of "WALK" and "DON'T WALK."
- She tried to put M&Ms in alphabetical order.

She was sooooo blonde ...
- She studied for a blood test.
- She sold her car to get gas money.
- When she missed bus #44 she took bus #22 twice instead.
- When she went to the airport and saw a sign that said, "Airport Left," she turned around and went home.

She was sooooo blonde ...
- When she heard that 90% of all crimes occur around the home, she moved.
- She thought if she spoke her mind, she'd be speechless.
- She thought that she could not use her AM radio in the evening.
- She thought Taco Bell was the Mexican phone company.

> *Everyone has a photographic memory.*
> *Some just don't have any film.*

✛✛✛ Stay! Stay! Do you hear me? ✛✛✛

A blonde pulled into into a crowded parking lot, parked, and rolled down her car windows so her Labrador Retriever stretched out on the back seat would have plenty of fresh air. She wanted to impress upon the dog that he must remain right there, so, she slowly walked backward away from the car, pointing her finger at the car and emphatically saying, "Now you stay. Do you hear me? Stay! Stay!"

The driver of a nearby car, perhaps noting that the woman was blonde, said. "Why don't you just put the car in park?"

Two blondes in another parking lot were trying to unlock the door of their Mercedes with a coat hanger. They tried and tried, but just couldn't get it unlocked. Then suddenly the blonde with the coat hanger stopped, looked up, and said, "Oh, no! It's starting to rain ... and the top is down!"

✛✛✛ Flying coach or first class? ✛✛✛

A blonde bought a coach fare plane ticket to Miami. But when she got on the plane, she sat down in the first class section. When a stewardess came around checking the tickets, she said to the blonde: "I'm sorry, this is a coach ticket and you are sitting in first class."

The blonde replied: "I'm not moving. I'm staying right here in this seat."

The stewardess reported this problem to the pilot ... and so the pilot came out and whispered something in the blonde's ear. Then she quietly got up and moved right back to the coach section.

The stewardess was very impressed and asked the pilot: "What did you say to her?"

The pilot said, "I just told her that first class wasn't going to Miami, only coach was."

Share some hearty laughter every day!

*Don't get smart with me, buster.
You're no more fittin' to be a station agent
than for goodness sake, that's all I hope,
and I'm just the girl who can do it, too.*

✧✧✧ To catch a thief ✧✧✧

Oscar drove his new Mercedes to his favorite sporting goods store and went in to do a little shopping. While he was looking around, a little blonde sales gal who knew Oscar well from his frequent visits to the store came running up to him yelling, "Oscar! Oscar! I just saw someone driving off with your new Mercedes."

"Good grief, didn't you try to stop him?"

"No," she said, "but I did get the license plate number."

✧✧✧ Blonde handy-woman ✧✧✧

A blonde decided to hire herself out as a "handy woman," so she started canvassing a nearby well-to-do neighborhood. She went to the front door of the first house and asked the owner if he might have any odd jobs that she could do.

"Well," said the homeowner, "you could paint my porch ... how much would you charge me?"

The blonde looked around and said, "How about $50?"

The man agreed and told her that the paint and other materials that she might need were in the garage. The man's wife overheard the conversation and said to her husband, "Does she realize that our porch goes all the way around the house?" The man replied, "Well she certainly should know that. She was standing on it."

A short time later, the blonde came to the door to collect her money.

"Finished already?" the husband asked. "Yes," the blonde replied, "and I had paint left over, so I gave it two coats."

Impressed, the man reached into his pocket for the $50 and handed it to her.

"And by the way," the blonde said, "It's not a Porsche, it's a Lexus."

Share some hearty laughter every day!

✦✦✦ Blonde officer stops blonde speeder ✦✦✦

As a young blonde was racing down the highway, a blonde police officer pulled her over for speeding. The officer said, "May I see your license?" The driver said, "What does it look like?" The officer said: "It's rectangular thing with a photo of you on it."

The blonde driver looked all through her handbag and finally pulled out her compact mirror and handed it to the officer.

The blonde officer opened it up, looked at it for a moment, and then said, "If you had told me that you were a police officer, I wouldn't have pulled you over."

> A blonde was worried
> that a mechanic might try to rip her off ...
> but she was relieved when he told her
> that all she needed was turn signal fluid.

✦✦✦ Small pink curtains ✦✦✦

A blonde woman went into a department store and told a salesman that she wanted to purchase a pair of pink curtains. The salesman showed her several different fabric choices and the blonde picked out a nice floral pattern.

The salesman asked, "What size do you need?"

The blonde replied: "15 inch."

The salesman said, "15 inch? ... I'm afraid we don't have any curtains that small. What room would this be for?"

The blonde replied, "It's not for a room, it's for my computer."

The salesman said, "For your computer? Miss, computers do not need curtains."

The blonde said: "Helloooooo ... I've got windows."

Rejoice! Clean Humor

Then there was the blonde ... who kept a lifesaving tool in her car that was designed to cut through a seatbelt if she ever got trapped in her car. She kept it in her trunk so no one would steal it.

Then there was the blonde ... overheard chatting with her friend in the cafeteria and expressing amazement that she got a sunburn while on her weekend excursion. She said, "I was driving in my convertible, but I didn't think that I would get sunburned because the car was moving."

Then there was the blonde ... talking with an airline passenger who couldn't find his luggage at the airport baggage area. He had gone to the lost luggage office and told the blonde working there that his bags never showed up. She smiled sweetly and said, "Don't worry. I am a trained professional and you are in good hands." Then, she asked: "Has your plane arrived yet?"

Then there was the blonde ... who called the customer service department and asked what hours they were open. The representative replied: "The number you called is open 24 hours-a-day, 7-days-a-week." She then asked: "Is that Eastern, Central, or Pacific time?"

✦✦✦ Progressive parenting ✦✦✦

Morris and Becky were thrilled when they learned that their long wait to adopt a baby had finally reached a happy conclusion. When the adoption center called and informed them that a sweet little Russian baby boy was now available for them, the couple agreed without hesitation go adopt him.

On their way home from the adoption center, they stopped by the local college to enroll in night courses. After filling out the enrollment form, the registration clerk asked, "What ever possessed you to decide to study Russian?"

The couple replied, "We just adopted a Russian baby and in a year or so when he begins to talk, we want to be able to understand him." No doubt you guessed, Morris and Becky are both blonde.

Share some hearty laughter every day!

✦✦✦ How to avoid losing your mind ✦✦✦

A blonde went to a supermarket to pick up some groceries. After she returned to her car, several people noticed her sitting in her car with the windows rolled up, with her eyes closed, and with both of her hands on the back of her head.

After about 15 minutes passed, one customer (who had noticed her before going into the store and saw her still sitting there holding the back of her head when he came back out of the store), became concerned and walked over closer to the car to investigate. He noticed that her eyes were now open, but she had a very strange look on her face.

So, the concerned gentleman asked the young lady if she was okay. She replied that she had been shot in the back of the head and had been holding her brains in for nearly an hour. Immediately, he called the paramedics. When they arrived, they had to break into the car, because the doors were locked and the young lady refused to move her hands from the back of her head. Once in the car, the paramedics discovered that the woman had a wad of bread dough on the back of her head.

It seems that a Pillsbury biscuit canister had exploded from the heat, making a loud noise that sounded like a gunshot, and the wad of dough had hit her in the back of her head. When she reached back to find out what it was, she felt the soft gooey dough and thought it was her brains. So she decided that she had to try to hold her brains in her head until help arrived.

---

*Do you know how can you tell
if a blonde has been using your computer?
There is whiteout all over the monitor.*

---

*Do you know why they never hire blondes as pharmacists?
It's because they keep breaking the prescription bottles
in the typewriters.*

✦✦✦ Blonde helicopter pilot ✦✦✦

A blonde pilot decided that she would like to learn how to fly a helicopter. So she went to the airport to rent one. The only one available was a solo-helicopter, but the instructor decided that he could let her take the copter up alone since she was, after all, a trained pilot, and he figured he could give her the additional instructions she might need by radio.

So, up she went ... to 1,000 feet ... and then to 2,000 feet. Everything was going smoothly as the instructor continued giving her instructions by radio.

But then, after she passed 3,000 feet, all of a sudden the helicopter began to descend very quickly. It skimmed the top of some trees and crash landed in some nearby woods.

The instructor jumped into his jeep and rushed out to see if the young lady was okay. As he came to the edge of the woods, he met her walking out, unharmed.

"What happened?" the instructor asked. "Everything seemed to be going so well until you reached 3,000 feet. What happened then?"

"Well," the blonde explained, "When I got up that high, it started to get cold, so I just turned off that big fan."

Then there was the blonde

... who went to the doctor complaining of pain. The doctor asked: "Where are you hurting?"

The blonde replied: "You have to help me, doctor. I hurt all over." The doctor said: "What do you mean, all over? Can you be a little more specific." The woman touched her right knee with her finger and yelled: "Ow, that hurts." Then she touched her left cheek and again yelled: "Ouch, that hurts too." Then she touched her right earlobe and cried: "Ow, even that hurts."

The doctor looked at her thoughtfully for a moment and asked: "Are you a natural blonde?" The young lady replied: "Why yes." The doctor said: "I thought so. You have a broken finger."

Share some hearty laughter every day!

✦✦ Blonde stewardess gets stuck in room ✦✦

An airline captain was breaking in a pretty new blonde stewardess. The route they were flying had a stay-over in another city. Upon their arrival the captain showed the stewardess the best place for airline personnel to eat, shop, and stay overnight.

The next morning as the pilot was preparing the crew for the day's route, he noticed the new stewardess was missing. He knew which room she was in at the hotel, so he called her to ask what happened to her. She answered the phone, crying, and said she couldn't get out of her room.

"You can't get out of your room?" the captain asked, "Why not?" The stewardess replied, "There are only three doors in here," she sobbed, "one is the bathroom, one is the closet, and one has a sign on it that says 'Do Not Disturb'."

✦✦ Wonderful new inventions by blondes ✦✦

- A water-proof towel
- Glow in the dark sunglasses
- Solar powered flashlights
- Submarine screen doors
- A book on how to read
- Inflatable dart boards
- A dictionary index
- Mechanical pencil sharpeners
- Powdered water
- Pedal-powered wheel chairs
- Waterproof tea bags
- Watermelon seed sorter
- Zero proof alcohol
- Skinless bananas
- Do-it-yourself road map
- Turnip ice cream
- Rolls Royce pickup truck
- Helicopter ejector Seat

✦✦✦ Blonde resurrects dead rabbit ✦✦✦

As a man was driving down a back country lane, he spotted a rabbit hopping across the road. He swerved to try to avoid hitting the rabbit, but the rabbit jumped right in front of the car and was hit.

Being a sensitive man who loved animals, the driver pulled over to the side of the road and got out to see if the rabbit was okay. To his great dismay, he saw that the rabbit was dead. He felt so awful about this that he began to cry.

Then a blonde woman came driving down that same road, saw the man crying, pulled over, stepped out of her car, and asked the man what was wrong.

"I feel terrible," he said, "I accidentally hit this little rabbit and killed it.

The blonde told the man not to worry, she knew what to do. She went to her car, opened the trunk, opened her luggage, and pulled out a can of hair spray. Then she walked over to the limp, dead rabbit, and sprayed the contents of the can on the rabbit.

Miraculously, the rabbit came to life, jumped up, waved its paw at the two people, and hopped on down the road. After hopping about ten feet, the rabbit stopped, turned around, waved at them again, and hopped down the road another 10 feet, turned, waved again, then hopped another 10 feet, turned and waved, and repeated this over and over again until it disappeared out of sight.

The man was astonished. He could not imagine what might have been in the blonde's spray can, so he asked her, "What in the world was in your spray can that you sprayed on that poor little rabbit that brought him back to life?"

The blonde turned the can around so the man could read the label. And there in giant letters it said:

"Hair spray -- restores life to dead hair and adds a permanent wave."

Share some hearty laughter every day!

✢✢✢ Blonde co-ed takes final exam ✢✢✢

As the blonde co-ed began to take her final exam *(which consisted entirely of "yes -or- no" questions)*, she took her seat in the classroom, stared at the exam for five minutes, and then in a moment of inspiration, took out her purse, removed a coin, and started tossing it and marking her answer sheet ... heads for yes and tails for no.

Within half an hour she completed the exam, while the rest of the class was still feverishly continuing to work.

So, since she had time left, she resumed flipping the coin again and again ... and quickly became very frustrated ... desperately flipping the coin faster and faster, mumbling and perspiring.

The instructor came over to her and asked if there was a problem.

She replied, "I finished this exam in half an hour, and now I'm rechecking my answers, but now they aren't coming out right."

**ILLITERATE?
WRITE FOR FREE HELP.**
ILLITERACY FOUNDATION
806 MAIN STREET

A blonde was feeding money into a coke machine
and had several cases of coke on the floor beside her.
Someone asked her:
"Why are you feeding all that money into that machine?"

The blonde replied:
"Are you kidding? ... I'm winning!"

✦ ✦ Creative answering machine messages ✦ ✦

- Hi. This is John's answering machine. He's not here ... but I'm open to suggestions.

- Hello. I'm David's answering machine. What are you?

- Suicide Hotline ... please hold.

- *(With a Clint Eastwood voice):* Go ahead ... make my day. Leave a message.

- Hi. Our answering machine is broken. This is the refrigerator speaking. Please speak slowly and I'll stick your message to myself with one of these magnets.

- Machine voice: Hello. This is Echo 5. You have reached the former telephone number of John Smith. I have taken over the functions of this inferior being. He has been saved to disk. If you would like to leave input for his file, do so at the tone.

- *(Rod Serling imitation)*: You're dazed, bewildered, trapped in a world without time, where sound collides with color and shadows explode. You see a sign ... this is no ordinary telephone answering device ... you have reached, "The Twilight Phone."

- This is not an answering machine. This is a telepathic thought-recording device. After the tone, think about your name, think about your reason for calling, and think about a number where I can reach you ... and I'll think about returning your call.

- The President is not in at this time. Please leave your name, number, and the name of the country you want us to invade.

- Hello you have reached the Van Buren residence. All of our operators are busy at the moment. Your call will be processed in the order it was received ... if you leave a message.

- Hello, this is ZKZK talk radio. You're on the air. What is your topic today?

Share some hearty laughter every day!

- This is a test of the Answering Machine Broadcast System. This is only a test.

- Thank you for calling Last Straw Chiropractic. We can't come to the phone right now because we are making adjustments. *(Break a few small twigs.)* Leave a message and we'll call you back as soon as we're finished here. *(Now break a bigger stick.)*

- You have reached the Strategic Air Command Nuclear Missile Storage Facility. At the tone, please leave your name, number, and target list. We will launch as soon as possible.

- Hi, this is George. Sorry I can't answer the phone right now. Leave a message and wait by the phone 'til I can call you back.

- Good day, Jim. Your contact is not available right now. Your mission, should you choose to accept it, is to leave your name, number, and a brief message at the tone. This tape will self-destruct in thirty seconds. Good Luck, Jim.

- All of our operators are currently busy. Please stay on the line, and your call will be answered in the order it was received. Thank you for holding. Your call is important to us. Please continue to hold. Or, if your emergency isn't too serious, leave a message and one of our crisis operators will call you back.

- After the message, please leave a tone.

- Hello, you have reached 555-1234. Our voice mail system is currently experiencing difficulties, so at the tone, please type your message on the keypad using the appropriate letters, and press the pound sign when finished.

- Congratulations! By correctly dialing 123-4567 you are eligible to leave a message. *(applause)* Now you can join the lucky few that have advanced to the next level. *(cheers)* At the sound of the tone, leave your name, number, and a brief message.

- Hello, you have reached Dave Johnson. At the tone, please enter your four digit PIN.

Rejoice! Clean Humor

- Thanks for calling Dial-A-Shrink. After the tone, please leave your name, number, and talk briefly about your childhood. I'll get back to you with my diagnosis as soon as possible.

- Hello. I'm not home right now but I can take a message. Hang on a second while I get a pencil. *(Open a drawer and shuffle stuff around.)* OK, please speak slowly so I can write this down.

- Hello. I would like to order two medium pepperoni pizzas please, with extra cheese. Oh, did I get the wrong number?

- *(Gameshow-announcer voice):* Hello, and welcome to Phone Tag. If you'd like to join the game, please leave your name and number ... and thanks again for playing Phone Tag.

- You are growing tired. Your eyelids are heavy. You feel very sleepy. You are gradually losing your willpower and ability to resist suggestions. When you hear the tone you will feel helplessly compelled to leave your name, number, and message.

- So. You've finally called. And I suppose you think I'll just be here for you. Well you're wrong. I gave up on you yesterday. Seventeen weeks was long enough to wait for you ... staring at the phone ... never going anywhere. Well I've had enough ... so I decided to get a real life. Now I am out there testing lint removers for Ralph Nader. So, please leave a message.

- *(Noble, aristocratic voice):* Yes, one million dollars could be yours ... **IF** you leave your name, number, and the reason why you want to join the ranks of The Rich and Famous.

- Hi, this is Bill. Thanks for calling during my spring pledge drive. A basic membership is only $30. Please wait for the tone, and thanks very much for your generous pledge.

- *(Jack Webb voice):* This is the city. I work here. I carry a tune. I was changing my name to protect my innocence when I got the call about a 411. It sounded like good information. But I need more. A name ... a number ... a FAX. Nothing but the FAX, ma'am. *(Hum the "Dragnet" theme - dum duh dum dum)*

Share some hearty laughter every day!

- Hi. I am not speaking to you right now. But you can talk to my answering machine without having to put up with any wise crack interruptions from me ... at least until I call you back.

- Sorry. You have reached an imaginary number. Please rotate your phone 90 degrees and try again.

- Knock, knock. *(... pause ... caller is thinking "Who's there?")* Isn't that *my* question? *(pause)* Please leave a message.

- *(Loud music playing in the background)* "Hello... HELLO??? I can't hear you. What? Oh ... we're not home ... please speak up.

- *Voice 1:* Answer the phone Hal, please.
  Voice 2: Sorry Dave, I can't do that.

- This answering machine message is for all you psychics out there .... *(long silence)* .... BEEP

- Hello. Welcome to the Psychiatric Hotline. If you are obsessive-compulsive, press 1 repeatedly. If you are co-dependent, please ask someone to press 2. If you have multiple personalities, please press 3, 4, 5 and 6. If you are paranoid-delusional, we know who you are and what you want, so just stay on the line until we can trace this call. If you are schizophrenic, listen carefully and a little voice will tell you which number to press. If you are manic-depressive, it doesn't matter which number you press. No one will answer.

- You have the right to remain silent. Everything you say will be recorded and will be used as information to call you back.

---

*My wife and I have come
to a perfect understanding:
I don't try to run her life,
and I don't try to run mine.*

✦ Epitaphs ✦ from cemetery gravestones

In a London, England cemetery:
    Ann Mann
    Here lies Ann Mann,
    Who lived an old maid
    But died an old Mann. -- Dec. 8, 1767

In a Ruidoso, New Mexico, cemetery:
    Here lies
    Johnny Yeast
    Pardon me
    For not rising.

In a Uniontown, Pennsylvania cemetery:
    Here lies the body
    of Jonathan Blake
    Stepped on the gas
    Instead of the brake.

In a Silver City, Nevada, cemetery:
    Here lays Butch,
    We planted him raw.
    He was quick on the trigger,
    But slow on the draw.

On a grave from the 1880's in Nantucket, Massachusetts
    Under the sod and under the trees
    Lies the body of Jonathan Pease.
    He is not here, there's only the pod:
    Pease shelled out and went to God.

Share some hearty laughter every day!

Lester Moore, a Wells, Fargo Co. station agent in the 1880's.
is buried in the Boot Hill Cemetery with this epitaph:
>Here lies Lester Moore
>Four slugs from a .44
>No Les No More.

A widow wrote this epitaph in a Vermont cemetery:
Sacred to the memory of my husband John Barnes
who died January 3, 1803
>His comely young widow, aged 23,
>has many qualifications of a good wife,
>and yearns to be comforted.

On Margaret Daniels grave at Hollywood Cemetery
in Richmond, Virginia:
>She always said her feet were killing her,
>but nobody believed her.

In a cemetery in Hartscombe, England
>On the 22nd of June
>Jonathan Fiddle
>Went out of tune.

Harry Edsel Smith of Albany, New York
>Looked up the elevator shaft to see if
>the car was on the way down. It was.

In a Thurmont, Maryland, cemetery
>Here lies an Atheist
>All dressed up and no place to go.

In a cemetery in England
>Remember man, as you walk by,
>As you are now, so once was I,
>As I am now, so shall you be,
>Remember this and follow me.

To which someone replied by writing on this tombstone
>To follow you I'll not consent,
>Until I know which way you went.

Rejoice! Clean Humor

✦✦✦ Church bulletin bloopers ✦✦✦

- The peacemaking meeting scheduled for today has been canceled due to a conflict.

- For those of you who have children and don't know it, we have a nursery downstairs.

- During the absence of our Pastor, we enjoyed the rare privilege of hearing a good sermon when J.F. Stubbs supplied our pulpit.

- Irving Benson and Jessie Carter were married on October 24 in the church. So ends a friendship that began in their school days.

- The Lutheran men's group will meet at 6 P.M. Steak, potatoes, green beans, and dessert will be served for a nominal feel.

- The church will host an evening of fine dining, superb entertainment, and gracious hostility.

- Potluck supper Sunday -- prayer and medication to follow.

- The ladies of the Church have cast off clothing of every kind. They may be seen in the basement on Friday afternoon.

- This evening, there will be a hymn sing in the park across from the Church. Bring a blanket and come prepared to sin.

- The Low Self Esteem Support Group will be meeting on Friday at 7 PM. Please use the back door.

- Weight Watchers will meet Monday at the First Presbyterian Church. Please use the double doors at the side entrance.

Share some hearty laughter every day!

✦✦✦ From the school of higher learning ✦✦✦

An eclectic collection gathered from a wide variety of sources, including some from history teacher and author Richard Lederer (from statements he gleaned from some of his students' essays), some Tina Mancuso reportedly collected from fifth and sixth grade test papers, and many other sources. Pay close attention to the hilarious spelling and misuse of some words to get the full effect.

- Ancient Egypt was inhabited by the mummies who wrote in hydraulics. They lived in the Sarah Dessert. The climate of the Sarah is such that the inhabitants have to live elsewhere.

- The Greeks were a highly sculptured people. Without them we wouldn't have history. The Greeks also had many myths. A myth is a female moth.

- Socrates was a famous Greek who went around giving people advice so they killed him. He died from an overdose of wedlock and after his death his career suffered a dramatic decline.

- In the Olympic games, the Greeks ran races, jumped, hurled biscuits, and threw the java.

- Eventually, the Romans conquered the Greeks. History calls them Romans because they never stayed very long in one place.

- Julius Caesar extinguished himself on the battlefields of Gaul. The Ides of March murdered him because they thought he was going to be made king. Dying, he gasped out: "Tee hee, Brutus."

- Nero was a cruel tyranny who would torture his subjects by playing the fiddle to them.

- Joan of Arc was burnt to a steak and then was later canonized by Bernard Shaw.

- In midevil times most people were alliterate. The greatest writer of the futile ages was Chaucer, who wrote many poems and verses and he also wrote literature.

- Gutenberg invented removable type and the Bible. Another important invention was the circulation of blood. Sir Walter Raleigh invented cigarettes and started smoking. Sir Francis Drake circumcised the world with a 100-foot clipper.

- The Bible is full of interesting caricatures. One of Adam and Eve's children, Cain asked: "Am I my brother's son?"

- The greatest writer of the Renaissance was William Shakespeare. He never made much money but is famous because of his plays. He wrote tragedies, comedies, and hysterectomies in Islamic pentameter. Romeo and Juliet are an example of a heroicouplet.

- Writing at the same time as Shakespeare was Miguel Cervantes. He wrote Donkey Hote. The next great author was John Milton. Milton wrote Paradise Lost. Then his wife died and he wrote Paradise Regained.

- America began during the Renaissance. Christopher Columbus was a great navigator who discovered America while cursing about the Atlantic. His ships were called the Nina, the Pinta, and the Santa Fe.

- Later, the Pilgrims crossed the ocean and this was called Pilgrim's Progress. The winter of 1620 was a hard one for the settlers. Many died and many babies were born. Captain John Smith was responsible for all this.

- One of the causes of the Revolutionary War was when the English put tacks in their tea. Also, the colonists would send their parcels through the post without stamps. But finally the colonists won the war and no longer had to pay for taxis.

- Delegates from the original 13 states formed the Contented Congress. Thomas Jefferson, a Virgin, and Benjamin Franklin were two singers of the Declaration of Independence. Franklin discovered electricity by rubbing two cats backwards. He also declared, "A horse divided against itself cannot stand." Franklin died in 1790 and is still dead.

Share some hearty laughter every day!

- The Constitution of the United States was adopted to secure domestic hostility. Under the constitution the people enjoyed the right to keep bare arms.

- Magna Carta provided that no free man should be hanged twice for the same offense.

- Martin Luther was nailed to the church door at Wittenberg.

- Lincoln's mother died in infancy and he was born in a log cabin which he built with his own hands.

- Question: What is one horsepower?
  Answer: One horsepower is the amount of energy it takes to drag a horse 500 feet in one second.

- They say the cause of perfume disappearing is evaporation. Evaporation gets blamed for a lot of things when people forget to put the top on.

- To most people solutions means finding the answers. But to chemists solutions are things that are still all mixed up.

- You can listen to thunder after lightening and tell how close you came to getting hit. If you don't hear it, you got hit, so never mind.

- Some people can tell what time it is by looking at the sun. But I have never been able to make out the numbers.

- In looking at a drop of water under a microscope, we find there are twice as many H's as O's.

A student was asked if he knew what the Roe vs. Wade decision was. He pondered this profound question for a few minutes and then said: "I think this was the decision George Washington made prior to crossing the Delaware."

Rejoice! Clean Humor

✦✦ Choice excerpts from actual exam papers ✦✦

1. Charles Darwin was a naturalist who wrote the organ of the species.
2. Evolution teaches us that reptiles came from amphibians by spontaneous generation and the study of rocks
3. The theory of evolution was greatly objected to because it made man think.
4. The three kinds of blood vessels are arteries, vanes, and caterpillars.
5. The dodo is a bird that is almost decent by now.
6. To remove air from a flask, fill it with water, tip the water out, and put the cork in quick before the air can get back in.
7. The process of turning steam back into water again is called conversation.
8. A magnet is something you find crawling all over a dead cat.
9. The Earth makes one resolution every 24 hours.
10. The cuckoo bird does not lay his own eggs.
11. To collect fumes of sulfur, hold a deacon over a flame in a test tube.
12. Parallel lines never meet, unless you bend one or both of them.
13. Algebraical symbols are used when you do not know what you are talking about.
14. Geometry teaches us to bisex angles.
15. A circle is a line that meets its other end without ending.
16. The pistol of a flower is its only protection against insects.
17. The moon is a planet just like the Earth, only it is even deader.
18. If you smell an odorless gas, it is probably carbon monoxide.
19. An example of animal breeding is the farmer who mated a bull that gave a lot of milk with a bull with good meat.
20. English sparrows and starlings eat the farmer's grain and soil his corpse.
21. By self-pollination, the farmer may get a flock of long-haired sheep.
22. If conditions are not favorable, bacteria go into a period of adolescence.
23. Dew is formed on leaves when the sun shines down on them and makes them perspire.
24. Vegetative propagation is the process by which one individual manufactures another individual by accident.

25. A super-saturated solution is a solution that holds more than it can hold.
26. A triangle that has an angle of 135 degrees is called an obscene triangle.
27. Blood flows down one leg and up the other.
28. The hookworm larvae enters the human body through the soul.
29. When you haven't got enough iodine in your blood you get a glacier.
30. It is a well-known fact that a deceased body harms the mind.
31. Humans are more intelligent than beasts because the human brains have more convulsions.
32. For fainting: rub the person's chest, or if it is a lady, rub her arm above the hand instead.
33. For fractures: to see if the limb is broken, wiggle it gently back and forth.
34. For dog bite: put the dog away for several days and if he has not recovered, then kill it.
35. For nosebleed: put the nose much lower than the body.
36. To remove dust from the eye, pull the eye down over the nose.
37. For head colds: use an agonizer to spray the nose until it drops in your throat.
38. For asphyxiation: apply artificial respiration until patient is dead.
39. Before giving a blood transfusion, make sure to find out if the blood is affirmative or negative.
40. Bar magnets have north poles and south poles, but horseshoe magnets have east poles and west poles.

✦✦✦ As easy as swatting flies ✦✦✦

A woman walked into the kitchen and saw her husband stalking around with a fly swatter. "What are you doing?" she asked.

"Hunting flies," He responded.

"Oh, killing any?" She asked.

"Yep, three males, two females," he replied.

Intrigued, she asked, "How can you tell which is which?"
He responded, "Three were on a beer can, two were on the phone."

Rejoice! Clean Humor

✦✦✦ Burma Shave Signs ✦✦✦
combine wisdom with humor

Don't lose your head
To gain a minute
You need your head
Your brains are in it.
*** Burma-Shave ***

Drove too long
Driver snoozing
What happened next
Is not amusing.
*** Burma-Shave ***

Brother speeder
Let's rehearse
All together
Good morning nurse.
*** Burma-Shave ***

Cautious rider
To her reckless dear
Let's have less bull
And a bit more steer.
*** Burma-Shave ***

The midnight ride
of Paul for beer
Led him to a warmer
Hemisphere.
*** Burma-Shave ***

Around the curve
Lickety-split
It's a beautiful car
Wasn't it?
*** Burma-Shave ***

No matter the price
No matter how new
The best safety device
In your car is you.
*** Burma-Shave ***

Both hands on the wheel
Both eyes on the road
That is the skillful
Driver's code.
*** Burma-Shave ***

Passing school zone
Take it slow
Let our little
Shavers grow.
*** Burma-Shave ***

The big blue tube's
Just like Louise
You get a thrill
From every squeeze.
*** Burma-Shave ***

Substitutes
Can let you down
Quicker than
A strapless gown.
*** Burma-Shave ***

Within this vale
Of toil and sin
Your head grows bald
But not your chin.
*** Burma-Shave ***

Share some hearty laughter every day!

Tho stiff the beard
That nature gave
It shaves like down
with *** Burma-Shave ***

Use this cream
A day or two
Then don't call her
She'll call you.
*** Burma-Shave ***

Prickly Pears
Are Picked for Pickles
But no Peach Picks
A Face that Prickles.
*** Burma-Shave ***

Ben met Anna
Made a hit
Neglected beard
Ben-Anna split.
*** Burma-Shave ***

Dinah doesn't
Treat him right
But if he'd shave
Dinah-might!
*** Burma-Shave ***

His tenor voice
She thought divine
'Til whiskers scratched
Sweet Adeline.
*** Burma-Shave ***

My job is keeping
Faces clean
And nobody knows
De stubble I've seen.
*** Burma-Shave ***

We've made grandpa
Look so trim
The local draft board
Is after him.
*** Burma-Shave ***

We're widely read
And often quoted
But it's shaves, not signs
For which we're noted.
*** Burma-Shave ***

Feel your face
As you ride by
Now don't you think
It's time to try
*** Burma-Shave ***

Toughest whiskers
In the town
We hold 'em up
You mow 'em down.
*** Burma-Shave ***

These signs are not
For laughs alone
The face they save
May be your own.
*** Burma-Shave ***

Farewell O verse
Along the road
How sad to see
You're out of mode.
*** Burma-Shave ***

So sad to know
The signs are all gone
But Burma-Shave mem'ries
Will always live on.

Rejoice! Clean Humor

✦✦✦ Can you hear me now? ✦✦✦

An elderly gentleman of 85 was concerned that his wife seemed to be getting hard of hearing. So one day he called her doctor to make an appointment to have her hearing checked.

The Doctor made an appointment for a hearing test in two weeks, and in the meantime, he told the elderly gentleman about a simple test he could do to give the doctor some idea of what the state of his wife's hearing problem might be.

"Here's what you do," the doctor said: "Start out about 40 feet away from her, and in a normal, conversational speaking tone, see if she can hear you when you speak to her. If not, move closer to about 30 feet, then 20 feet, and so on until you get a response."

So, that evening, while his wife was in the kitchen cooking dinner, and he was in the living room, he said to himself, "Okay, I'm about 40 feet away, so let's see what happens."

In a normal tone of voice, he asked his wife, 'Honey, what's for supper?" … No response.

So, he moved closer toward the kitchen, to about 30 feet away from his wife and again said, "Honey, what's for supper?"

Still no response.

So, he went into the dining room right next to the kitchen, about 20 feet from his wife and again said, "Honey, what's for supper?" Again he got no response, so he walked to the kitchen door, just 10 feet away and again said, "Honey, what's for supper?"

Again, no response. So he walked right up directly behind her and for the fourth time said, "Honey, what's for supper?"

Now his sweet wife, with just a little touch of exasperation in her voice, said: "For goodness sake Earl … for the fourth time …

We are having CHICKEN!"

Share some hearty laughter every day!

> *Cardiologist's diet:*
> *If it tastes good, spit it out.*

✦✦✦ So ... what foods are safe to eat? ✦✦✦

Can't eat beef, risks mad cow disease ...
Can't eat chicken, risks bird flu ...
Can't eat eggs, risks salmonella poisoning ...
Can't eat pork, fears that bird flu will infect piggies ...
Can't eat fish ... heavy metals in the water has poisoned their meat

That leaves chocolate. Chocolate is a vegetable.
Chocolate is derived from cocoa beans, and bean = vegetable.

Sugar is derived from either sugar cane or sugar beets.
Both sugar cane and sugar beets are in the vegetable category.
Therefore, chocolate is a vegetable.

Chocolate candy bars also contain milk, which is a dairy product. Therefore, candy bars are a health food. Moreover, chocolate-covered raisins, cherries, orange slices, and strawberries all count as fruit, so you can eat as many of them as you want.

Finally ... please remember this ... the word "stressed" spelled backward is "desserts." To reduce stress, just eat more desserts.

✦✦✦ fi yuo cna raed tihs ✦✦✦
yuo hvae a sgtrane mnid too

Cna yuo raed tihs? 55 plepoe out of 100 can.
i cdnuolt blveiee taht I cluod aulaclty uesdnatnrd waht I was rdanieg. The phaonmneal pweor of the hmuan mnid, aoccdrnig to a rscheearch at Cmabrigde Uinervtisy, it dseno't mtaetr in waht oerdr the ltteres in a wrod are, the olny iproamtnt tihng is taht the frsit and lsat ltteer be in the rghit pclae. The rset can be a taotl mses and you can sitll raed it whotuit a pboerlm. Tihs is bcuseae the huamn mnid deos not raed ervey lteter by istlef, but the wrod as a wlohe. Azanmig huh? yaeh and I awlyas tghuhot slpeling was ipmorantt.

✦✦✦ Classic classified ads ✦✦✦

Wedding dress for sale: Worn once by mistake.

Free Puppies: 1/2 Cocker Spaniel, 1/2 sneaky neighbor's dog.

Free German Shepherd: 85 lbs. Neutered. Speaks German.

Dog for sale: Eats anything and is fond of children.

Nordic Track: $300 Hardly used ... call Chubby

Open house - Body Shapers Toning Salon
Free coffee & donuts

Georgia Peaches: California grown - 89 cents lb.

Joining nudist colony: Must sell washer and dryer $300

Auto Repair Service. Free pick-up and delivery.
Try us once, you'll never go anywhere again.

Our experienced mom will care for your child.
Fenced yard, meals, and smacks included.

Man wanted to work in dynamite factory.
Must be willing to travel.

Stock up and save. Limit: one.

Semi-Annual after-Christmas Sale.

3-year old teacher needed for pre-school.
Experience preferred.

Mixing bowl set designed to please a cook
with round bottom for efficient beating.

Girl wanted to assist magician in cutting-off-head illusion.
Blue Cross and salary.

Share some hearty laughter every day!

Exercise equipment:
Queen size mattress & box springs $175.

Tired of cleaning yourself. Let me do it.

For Rent: 6-room hated apartment.

Work wanted: Honest man. Will take anything.

Used Cars: Why go elsewhere to be cheated.
Come here first.

Amana washer $100.
Owned by clean bachelor who seldom washed.

We do not tear your clothing with machinery.
We do it carefully by hand.

Have several very old dresses
from grandmother in beautiful condition.

Have your home exterminated. Get rid of aunts.
Zap does the job in 24 hours.

Tired of working for only $9.75 per hour?
We offer profit sharing and flexible hours.
Starting pay: $7 - $9 per hour.

---

83 Toyota hunchback $2000

Ground beast: 99 cents lb.

Shakespeare's Pizza - free chopsticks

Hummels - largest selection ever
"If it's in stock, we have it!"

Bill's Septic Cleaning Service:
"We haul American made products"

✦✦✦ A woman's revenge ✦✦✦

After folding the items the woman wanted to purchase, I asked, "Cash, check or charge?" As she looked through her purse to find her wallet, she set a TV remote control on the counter.

Unable to contain my curiosity, I said, "Do you always carry your TV remote with you?" She replied, "No, but my husband refused to come shopping with me, so I figured this was the most evil thing I could legally do to him."

---

*The reason a woman's mind
is a lot cleaner than a man's
is because she changes it more often.*

✦✦✦ Pastoral visit ✦✦✦

A new pastor went out visiting his parishioners. At one house it seemed obvious that someone was at home, but no answer came to his repeated knocks at the door. So he took out his card, wrote Revelation 3:20 on the back, and stuck it in the door.

The next Sunday, when the offering was processed following the service, he found that his card had been returned with this verse added on the card: Genesis 3:10.

Reaching for his Bible to check out the citations, he broke up in gales of laughter.

Revelation 3:20 begins: "Behold, I stand at the door and knock."

Genesis 3:10 reads: "I heard your voice in the garden and I was afraid for I was naked."

---

*Families are like fudge.
Mostly sweet, with a few nuts.*

Share some hearty laughter every day!

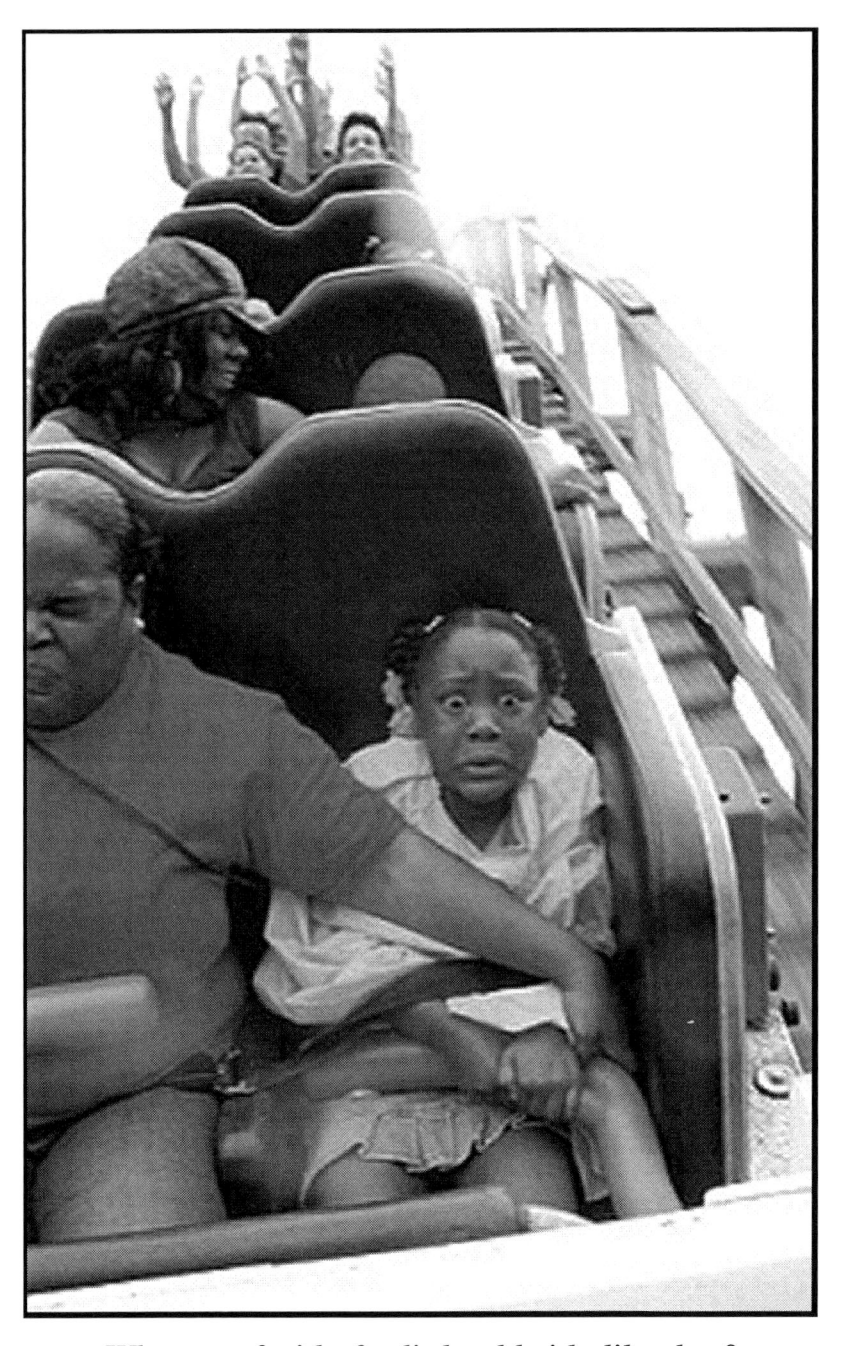

*Who me afraid of a little old ride like that?
Certainly not. I've done much wilder than that before.*

Rejoice! Clean Humor

✦✦✦ Clever translations ✦✦✦

New York magazine has run a contest in which contestants take a well-known foreign language expression, change a single letter, and provide a definition for the new expression. Following are some all time favorite winners.

Harlez-vous français?
CAN YOU DRIVE A FRENCH MOTORCYCLE?

Cogito Eggo Sum.
I THINK; THEREFORE I AM A WAFFLE.

Rigor morris.
THE CAT IS DEAD.

Repondez-vous s'il vous plaid.
HONK IF YOU'RE SCOTTISH.

Que sera serf.
LIFE IS FEUDAL.

Posh mortem.
DEATH STYLES OF THE RICH AND FAMOUS.

Pro Bozo publico
SUPPORT YOUR LOCAL CLOWN.

Haste cuisine.
FAST FRENCH FOOD.

Veni, vidi, vice.
I CAME, I SAW, I PARTIED.

Mazel ton.
TONS OF LUCK.

Aloha oy.
LOVE; GREETINGS; FAREWELL;
FROM SUCH A PAIN YOU SHOULD NEVER KNOW.

Share some hearty laughter every day!

Visa la France.
DON'T LEAVE YOUR CHATEAU WITHOUT IT.

L'état, c'est moo.
I'M BOSSY AROUND HERE.

Cogito, ergo spud.
I THINK, THEREFORE I YAM.
(OK, more than 1 letter.)

Veni, vidi, velcro
I CAME, I SAW, I STUCK AROUND.
(OK, another exception.)

✣✣✣ How well does cold water clean? ✣✣✣

A man went to visit his 90 year old grandfather in a secluded, rural area of the state. The next morning, his grandfather prepared a breakfast of eggs and bacon. The man noticed a film-like substance on his plate, so he asked his grandfather, "Are these plates clean?"

His grandfather said, "Those plates are as clean as cold water can get them, so you just go on and finish your meal."

At lunch time, his grandfather made hamburgers and the grandson noticed tiny specks around the edge of his plate that looked like dried egg yokes. So again he asked, "Are you sure these plates are clean?"

Without looking up from his lunch, grandfather said, "I told you before, those dishes are as clean as cold water can get them. Now just eat your lunch and don't ask me about this anymore."

Later that afternoon, as the grandson headed out to the mailbox to get the newspaper, the dog started to growl at him and wouldn't let him pass. He said: "Grandad, your dog won't let me out."

Without taking his eyes off of the exciting football game he was watching, his grandfather shouted, "Coldwater, move."

✦✦✦ Actual tech-support calls ✦✦✦

Tech support: What kind of computer do you have?
Female customer: A white one …

Customer: Hi, this is Maureen. I can't get my diskette out.
Tech support: Have you tried pushing the Button?
Customer: Yes, I have, but it's really stuck.
Tech support: That doesn't sound good; I'll make a note.
Customer: No, wait a minute … I hadn't inserted it yet … it's still on my desk … sorry …

Tech support: How can I help you?
Customer: I can't print.
Tech support: Would you please click on "Start" and …
Customer: Listen pal … don't start getting technical on me. I'm not Bill Gates.

Customer: Hi, this is Martha calling and I am unable to print. Every time I try, it says 'Can't find printer.' I have even moved the printer and placed it directly in front of the monitor, but the computer still says he can't find it.

Customer: I have problems printing in red.
Tech support: Do you have a color printer?
Customer: Aaaah ……………… thank you.

Tech support: What's on your monitor now, ma'am?
Customer: A teddy bear my boyfriend bought for me at Woolies.

Customer: My keyboard is not working anymore.
Tech support: Are you sure it's plugged into the computer?
Customer: No. I can't get behind the computer to check.
Tech support: Well, pick up your keyboard and walk back 10 steps.
Customer: Okay, I've done that.
Tech support: Did the keyboard come with you?
Customer: Yes
Tech support: That means the keyboard is not plugged in. Do you have another keyboard there?
Customer: Yes, there's another one … Ah … this one does work.

Share some hearty laughter every day!

Tech support: Click the 'my computer' icon on the left of the screen.
Customer: Your left or my left?

Tech support: Your password is the small letter "b" as in boy, a capital letter Z as in Zebra, and the number 7.
Customer: Is that 7 in capital letters?

Customer: I can't get on the Internet.
Tech support: Are you sure you used the right password?
Customer: Yes, I'm sure. I watched my colleague do it.
Tech support: Can you tell me what the password was?
Customer: Five asterisks.

Tech support: How may I help you?
Customer: I'm writing my first e-mail.
Tech support: OK, and what seems to be the problem?
Customer: Well, I have the letter 'a' in the address, but how do I get the circle around it?

A woman customer called about a problem with her printer.
Tech support: Are you running it under windows?
Customer: "No, my desk is next to the door, but that is a good point. The man sitting in the cubicle next to me is under a window, and his printer is working fine."

✦✦✦ Murphy's laws of computing ✦✦✦

- ❖ If at first you don't succeed, blame your computer.
- ❖ The #1 cause of computer problems is computer solutions.
- ❖ When you get to the point where you are beginning to understand your computer, it is undoubtedly obsolete.
- ❖ A complex system that does not work is invariably found to have evolved from a simpler system that worked just fine.
- ❖ For every action, there is an equal and opposite malfunction.
- ❖ A computer program will always do what you tell it to do, but rarely what you want it to do.
- ❖ When computing, whatever happens, behave as though you meant it to happen.
- ❖ He who laughs last probably made a back-up.

✦✦✦ Give me back my dog ✦✦✦

A shepherd was herding his flock in a remote pasture when a brand-new BMW roared out of a dust cloud toward him. The driver, a young man in an expensive suit and Ray Ban sunglasses leaned out the window and asked the shepherd, "If I tell you exactly how many sheep you have in your flock, will you give me one?"

The shepherd looked at the flashy yuppie, then looked at his peacefully grazing flock and calmly answered, "Sure. Why not?"

The yuppie parked his car, whipped out his notebook computer, connected it to his cell phone, surfed to a NASA page on the internet, where he called up a GPS satellite navigation system to get an exact fix on his location. He then fed that information to another NASA satellite that scanned the area to create an ultra-high-resolution photo. He then opened that digital photo in Photoshop and exported it to an image processing facility in Hamburg, Germany.

Within seconds, he received an email on his Palm Pilot telling him the image was processed, so he accessed an SQL database through an ODBC connected spreadsheet with hundreds of highly complex formulas, uploaded all this data via an email to his Blackberry and in seconds received a response that he printed out in full-color as a 150-page report on his miniature HP LaserJet printer. He then turned to the shepherd and said, "You have exactly 1586 sheep."

"That's correct. So, I guess you can take one of my sheep." the shepherd said. He watched the yuppie select one of his animals and looked on amused as he stuffed it into the trunk of his car. Then the shepherd said to the young man, "Hey, if I can tell you exactly what your business is, will you give back what you took?"

The young man thought for a second and said, "Okay, why not?"

"You're a consultant." said the shepherd.

"Wow, that's correct," said the yuppie. "How did you guess that?"

"No guessing required." answered the shepherd. "You showed up here even though nobody called you; you wanted to get paid for an answer I already knew, to a question I never asked, and you don't know anything about my business ... so give me back my dog."

Share some hearty laughter every day!

The sign above may be a little confusing, but that is no excuse to just create your own entrance.

Rejoice! Clean Humor

✦✦✦ Disorder in the court ✦✦✦

Actual quotes of questions and answers recorded word for word by court reporters who had the torment of trying to stay calm and keep from cracking up while these exchanges were taking place.

Attorney: What is your date of birth?
Witness: July 15th.
Attorney: What year?
Witness: Every year.

Attorney: How was your first marriage terminated?
Witness: By death.
Attorney: And by whose death was it terminated?

Attorney: Your youngest son, the twenty-year-old, how old is he?

Attorney: Does Myasthenia Gravis affect your memory at all?
Witness: Yes.
Attorney: And in what ways does it affect your memory?
Witness: I forget.
Attorney: You forget? Can you give us an example of something that you have forgotten?

Attorney: How old is your son, the one living with you?
Witness: Thirty-eight or thirty-five, I can't remember which.
Attorney: How long has he lived with you?
Witness: Forty-five years.

Attorney: Do you know if your daughter has ever been involved in voodoo?
Witness: We both do.
Attorney: Voodoo?
Witness: We do.
Attorney: You do?
Witness: Yes, voodoo.

Attorney: So the date of conception *(of the baby)* was August 8th?
Witness: Yes.
Attorney: And what were you doing at that time?

Share some hearty laughter every day!

Attorney: What gear were you in at the moment of the impact?
Witness: Gucci sweats and Reeboks.

Attorney: She had three children, right?
Witness: Yes.
Attorney: How many were boys?
Witness: None.
Attorney: Were there any girls?

Attorney: Can you describe the individual?
Witness: He was about medium height and had a beard.
Attorney: Was this a male or a female?

Attorney: Is your appearance here this morning pursuant to a deposition notice that I sent to your attorney?
Witness: No, this is how I dress when I go to work.

Attorney: Doctor, before you performed this autopsy, did you check for a pulse?
Witness: No.
Attorney: Did you check for blood pressure?
Witness: No.
Attorney: Did you check for breathing?
Witness: No.
Attorney: So, it is possible that the patient was alive when you began the autopsy?
Witness: No.
Attorney: How can you be so sure, doctor?
Witness: Because his brain was in a jar sitting on my desk.

✦✦✦ Marriage seminar ✦✦✦

While attending a Marriage Seminar, Tom and his wife listened to the instructor explain, "It is essential that husbands and wives know the things that are really important to each other." Then he said to the men in the audience, "For example, can you men describe your wife's favorite flower?"

At this point, Tom leaned over, gently touched his wife's arm, and whispered, "It's Pillsbury, isn't it?"

Rejoice! Clean Humor

✧✧✧ No nursing home in my future ✧✧✧

While on a cruise a while back, at dinner my wife and I noticed an elderly lady sitting alone in the dining room. We also noticed that all the ship's staff, officers, waiters, busboys, and other staff personnel seemed very familiar with this lady.

So I asked our waiter who the lady was, thinking that perhaps her family owned this cruise line, but he said that he only knew that she had been on board for the last four cruises, back to back.

As we left the dining room one evening I caught her eye and stopped to say hello. As we chatted, I said, "I understand you've been on this ship for the last four cruises." "Yes," she replied, "that is true." I said, "You must really enjoy cruising a great deal ..." Without hesitating, she said, "It's cheaper than a nursing home."

Makes perfect sense. So, when I get old and feeble, perhaps I'll follow her example and just get on a Princess Cruise Ship instead of going to a nursing home. The average cost for a nursing home is now more than $200 per day. I checked on cruise reservations and found that I can get a senior discount and repeat traveler price of only $135 per day ... so that leaves $65 a day for:

1. Gratuities are only $10 per day, and for an extra $5, the entire staff will be scrambling to serve my every need.
2. I will have as many as 10 meals a day provided -- even with room service and breakfast in bed every day of the week.
3. They provide free toothpaste, razors, soap, and shampoo.
4. Clean sheets and towels every day, without even asking.
5. Need a light bulb or mattress replaced? No Problem. They will promptly fix everything and apologize for your inconvenience.
6. They treat you like a valued customer, not like a patient.
7. And, I will get to meet new people every 7 or 14 days.
8. There are as many as three swimming pools, a workout room, free washers and dryers, and live entertainment every night.
9. If you fall in the nursing home and break a hip you are on Medicare. If you fall and break a hip on a cruise ship they will upgrade you to a suite for the rest of your life. And when you die, they can just dump you over the side at no charge.

Share some hearty laughter every day!

✦✦✦ Answers from traffic school exams ✦✦✦

The following is a sampling of actual answers received on exams given by the California Dept. of Transportation's traffic school.

Q: What is the difference between a flashing red traffic light and a flashing yellow traffic light?
A: The color.

Q: Who has the right of way when four cars approach a four-way stop at the same time?
A: The pick up truck with the gun rack and the bumper sticker saying, "Guns don't kill people. I do."

Q: When driving through fog, what should you use?
A: Your car.

Q: What are some points to remember when passing or being passed?
A: Make eye contact and wave "hello" if she is cute.

Q: What changes would occur in your lifestyle if you could no longer drive lawfully?
A: I would be forced to drive unlawfully.

✦✦✦ Think a gallon of gas is expensive? ✦✦✦
This will put things in perspective:

Diet Snapple	16 oz $1.29	=	$ 10.32 per gallon
Lipton Ice Tea	16 oz $1.19	=	$ 9.52 per gallon
Gatorade	20 oz $1.59	=	$ 10.17 per gallon
Ocean Spray	16 oz $1.25	=	$ 10.00 per gallon
Brake Fluid	12 oz $3.15	=	$ 33.60 per gallon
Vick's Nyquil	6 oz $8.35	=	$178.13 per gallon
Pepto Bismol	4 oz $3.85	=	$123.20 per gallon
Whiteout	7 oz $1.39	=	$ 25.42 per gallon
Scope	1.5 oz $0.99	=	$ 84.48 per gallon
Evian water	9 oz $1.49	=	$ 21.19 per gallon

So, the next time you're at the pump, be glad your car doesn't run on water, Scope, Whiteout, Pepto Bismal, or Nyquil.

Rejoice! Clean Humor

✦✦ Logical answers to key health questions ✦✦

Q: Is it true that cardiovascular exercise can prolong life?
A: Don't be silly. Your heart is only good for so many beats and that's it. So don't waste any precious heartbeats on exercise. Everything wears out eventually. Speeding up your heart will not make you live longer. That's like saying you can extend the life of your car by driving it faster. Want to live longer? Take a nap.

Q: Should I cut down on meat and eat more fruits and vegetables?
A: You must understand logistical efficiencies. What does a cow eat? Hay and corn. And what are these? Vegetables. Therefore, steak is nothing more than an efficient mechanism of delivering vegetables to your system. Beef is also a good source of field grass, a green leafy vegetable. And a pork chop can give you 100% of your recommended daily allowance of vegetable slop.

Q: Are beer and wine bad for me?
A: Look, this goes to the earlier point about fruits and vegetables. As we all know, scientists divide everything in the world into three categories: animal, mineral, and vegetable. We all know that beer and wine are not animal or mineral, so that only leaves one thing, right? My advice: Have a burger and a beer or glass of wine and enjoy your vegetables.

Q: What are some of the advantages of participating in a regular exercise program?
A: I can't think of a single one. My philosophy: No Pain … Good.

Q: Aren't fried foods bad for you?
A: You're not listening. Foods are fried in vegetable oil now, aren't they? So how could getting more vegetables be bad for you?

Q: Will sit-ups help me avoid getting soft around the middle?
A: Definitely not. When you exercise a muscle, it gets bigger, right? You should only do sit-ups if you want a bigger stomach.

Q: Is chocolate bad for me?
A: Are you crazy? HELLO … Cocoa beans = another vegetable. Chocolate is simply the best feel-good food there is.

Share some hearty laughter every day!

✦✦✦ Doctor tales ✦✦✦

A man came into the ER and yelled, "My wife is about to have a baby outside in the cab." So I grabbed my stuff, rushed out to the cab, lifted the lady's dress, and began to take off her underwear. Suddenly I noticed that there were several cabs ... and I was in the wrong one. --Dr. Mark MacDonald

While performing a physical, including a visual acuity test, I placed the patient twenty feet from the chart and began, "Cover your right eye with your hand." He read the 20/20 line perfectly. "Now your left." Again, a flawless read. "Now both." Silence. The patient could not even read the large E on the top line. I turned around and saw that he had done exactly what I had asked. There he stood with both eyes covered. I was laughing too hard to finish the exam. --Dr. Matthew Theodropolous

During a patient's two week follow-up appointment, he informed me that he was having trouble with one of his medications. "Which one?" I asked. "The patch. The nurse told me to put on a new one every six hours, and I'm running out of places to put it." When I had him undress, I couldn't believe what I saw. Yes, the man had more than fifty medicated patches covering his body. So, we have now revised the instructions to include removing the old patches before applying a new one. --Dr. Rebecca St. Clair

While acquainting myself with a new elderly patient, I asked, "How long have you been bedridden?" With a rather startled look of confusion she finally answered ... "Why, not for about twenty years when my husband was alive." --Dr. Steven Swanson

---

Genius home builders: Two men went to a lumberyard, one went inside and said, "We need some four-by-twos." The clerk said, "You mean two-by-fours, don't you?" The man said, "I'll go check." He returned and said, "Yeah, I meant two-by-fours." So the clerk said, "Okay. How long do you need them?" The customer paused again and said, "I'd better go check." Seconds later, he returned and said, "A long time. We're gonna build a house."

Rejoice! Clean Humor

✦✦✦ Safe driver awards ✦✦✦

Driving to the office this morning on the Interstate, I looked over to my left and there was a woman in a brand new Cadillac going 65 miles per hour with her face up really close to her rear view mirror putting on her eyeliner.

I looked away for a second, and when I looked back she was halfway over into my lane, still working on her makeup.

Now, being a man, I don't scare easily, but she scared me so much that I dropped my electric shaver, which knocked the donut out of my other hand. And in all the confusion of trying to keep my car straight using my knees against the steering wheel, I knocked my cell phone away from my ear and it fell into the coffee between my legs, which splashed out some hot coffee that soaked my trousers, burned my legs, ruined my phone, and thereby disconnected a very important phone call that I had been on.

For crying out loud, what incredible problems these careless women drivers are causing all of us careful men.

✦✦✦ Did you ever wonder why? ✦✦✦

Why women can't put on mascara with their mouth closed?
Why abbreviated is such a long word?
Why doctors call what they do practice?
Why is it that to stop Windows, you have to click on "Start?"
Why the man who invests all your money is called a broker?
Why is the time of day with the slowest traffic called rush hour?
Why the sun lightens our hair, but darkens our skin?
Why don't sheep shrink when it rains?
Why you never see the headline "Psychic Wins Lottery?"
Why are they called apartments when they are all stuck together?
Why, if flying is so safe, do they call the airport the terminal?
Why lemon juice is made with artificial flavor,
     and dishwashing liquid is made with real lemons?
Since "con" is the opposite of "pro," why did our country have to end up with a Congress with two groups constantly in opposition to each other instead of a legislative body named "Progress?"

Share some hearty laughter every day!

Rejoice! Clean Humor

✦✦ Deep philosophical questions to ponder ✦✦

? Can a hearse carrying a corpse drive in the carpool lane?

? How important does a person have to be before they can be considered assassinated instead of just murdered?

? Who was the first person to look at a cow and say, "I think I'll squeeze those dangly things and drink whatever comes out?"

? If Jimmy cracks corn and no one cares, why is there a song about him?

? Why does a doctor leave the room while you get undressed if he or she is going to come back in to examine you naked anyway?

? Why do people point to their wrist to ask for the time, but no one ever points to their crotch to ask where the bathroom is?

? Why do people pay to go to the top of tall skyscrapers and then put money in binoculars to look down at things on the ground?

? Can blind people see their dreams? In fact, can they even dream?

? If Wile E. Coyote had enough money to buy all that Acme stuff, why didn't he just buy dinner?

? Why is a person whose profession is giving investment advice called a 'Broker'?

? Why is it that if you blow in a dog's face, he gets mad at you; but if you take him on a car ride and he puts his head out the window, he is happy to have the wind blow in his face.

? Why is it that when someone tells you that there are over a billion stars in the universe, you believe them. But if they tell you some paint is wet, you have to touch it to make sure?

? If a man is all alone talking out in a forest and no woman is there to hear him, is he still wrong?

Share some hearty laughter every day!

- **?** Why do you "put in your two cents worth" but you only get a "penny for your thoughts?" Where does that extra penny go?

- **?** Since bread is square, why is sandwich meat round?

- **?** Why does a round pizza come in a square box?

- **?** What disease did cured ham have before it was cured?

- **?** Why is it that people say they "slept like a baby" when babies wake up every two hours?

- **?** If a deaf person has to go to court, is it still called a hearing?

- **?** Why are people *in* a movie, but *on* TV?

- **?** What do you call male ballerinas?

- **?** How hungry was the first person who opened an oyster, took one look at that slimy lump, and still ate it?

- **?** Why do they call it the Department of Interior when they are in charge of everything outdoors?

- **?** Why is it that you keep junk for years and years, but within three days after you throw it away, you need it?

- **?** If money doesn't grow on trees then why do banks have branches?

- **?** How come we choose between only two people for President but choose from 50 contestants for Miss America?

- **?** Why is it that children are prohibited from reading a Bible in school, but Bibles are given to prisoners in prison?

---

*Finally ... why is it that
brain cells come and brain cells go,
but fat cells seem to hang around forever.*

Rejoice! Clean Humor

✦✦✦ Notes children wrote to their pastors ✦✦✦

Dear Pastor, I know God loves everybody, but He never met my sister. Sincerely, Arnold, age 8

Dear Pastor, Please say in your sermon that Peter Peterson has been a good boy all week. I am Peter Peterson. Pete, age 9

Dear Pastor, My father should be a minister. Every day he gives us a sermon about something. Robert, age 11

Dear Pastor, I'm sorry I can't leave more money in the plate, but my father didn't give me a raise in my allowance. Could you have a sermon about a raise in my allowance? Love, Patty, age 10

Dear Pastor, I think a lot more people would come to your church if you moved it to Disneyland. Loreen, age 9

Dear Pastor, I hope to go to heaven some day but later than sooner. Love, Ellen, age 9

Dear Pastor, Please say a prayer for our Little League team. We need God's help or a new pitcher. Thank you. Alexander, age 10

Dear Pastor, My father says I should learn the Ten Commandments. But I don't think I want to because we have enough rules already in my house. Joshua, age 10

Dear Pastor, Are there any devils on the earth? I think there may be one in my class. Carla, age 10

Dear Pastor, How does God know the good people from the bad people? Do you tell Him or does He just read about it in the newspapers? Sincerely, Marie, age 9

Dear Pastor, I liked your sermon on Sunday. Especially when it was finished. Ralph, age 11

> *Always keep your words soft and sweet,*
> *in case you have to eat them.*

Share some hearty laughter every day!

✦✦✦ English is a crazy, illogical language ✦✦✦

There is no egg in eggplant, no ham in hamburger, and neither apple nor pine in a pineapple. And quicksand works slowly.

English muffins were not invented in England, nor were French fries invented in France. Sweetmeats are candies, while sweetbreads *(which are neither sweet nor bread)*, are meat.

Boxing rings are square and a guinea pig is not a pig and it is not from Guinea. Writers write but fingers don't fing, grocers don't groce, and hammers don't ham.

The plural of tooth is teeth, so why isn't the plural of booth beeth? The plural of goose is geese. Why isn't the plural of moose meese? And why is there one index, but two indices?

Doesn't it seem crazy that you can make amends, but not one amend?

If you have a bunch of odds and ends and get rid of all but one of them, what do you call it?

We say teachers taught, so why don't we say preachers praught? If a vegetarian eats vegetables, what do a humanitarians eat?

How come one recites a play and plays at a recital? Ships by truck and sends cargo by ship? Has a nose that runs and feet that smell?

How can a slim chance and a fat chance be the same, while a wise man and a wise guy are opposites?

How can it be that a house can burn up as it burns down? And you fill out a form by filling it in? And an alarm goes off by going on?

Why is it that when the stars are out, they are visible, but when the lights are out, they are invisible?

And by the way, why doesn't Buick rhyme with Quick?

The list of crazy, illogical English words almost seems endless.

Rejoice! Clean Humor

For example, consider these curious combinations:

- The bandage was wound around the wound.
- The farm was used to produce produce.
- The dump was so full that it had to refuse more refuse.
- We must polish the Polish furniture.
- He could lead if he would get the lead out.
- The soldier decided to desert his dessert in the desert.
- There is no time like the present to present the present.
- A bass was painted on the head of the bass drum.
- When shot at, the dove dove into the bushes.
- I did not object to the object.
- The insurance was invalid for the invalid.
- There was a row among the oarsmen about how to row.
- They were too close to the door to close it.
- The buck does funny things when the does are present.
- A seamstress and a sewer fell down into the sewer.
- To help with planting, the farmer taught his sow to sow.
- The wind was too strong to wind the sail.
- After a number of injections my jaw got number.
- Upon seeing the tear in the painting, I shed a tear.
- I had to subject the subject to a series of tests.
- How can I intimate this to my most intimate friend?

✦✦✦ Letter home from Marine boot camp ✦✦✦

Dear Ma and Pa:

I am fine. Hope you are. Tell my brothers Walt and Elmer that the Marine Corp sure beats workin' for old man Minch. I was restless at first because you got to stay in bed till nearly 6 AM, but I'm finally gettin' used to this sleepin' in late.

Tell Walt and Elmer all you have to do before breakfast is smooth your cot and shine some things. No hogs to slop, no feed to pitch,

Share some hearty laughter every day!

no mash to mix, wood to split, or fire to lay. Almost nothin' to do. We have to shave, but it ain't so bad 'cause they got warm water.

Breakfast is strong on trimmin's like fruit juice, cereal, bacon, eggs, and biscuits; but kind of weak on chops, potatoes, ham, steak, fried eggplant, pie, and other regular food. But tell Walt and Elmer you can always sit by them city boys that jus' live on coffee. Their food plus yours holds ya till noon when you git fed again.

Them city boys sure can't walk much. We go on 'route' marches, which the platoon sergeant says are long walks to harden us. But if he thinks that, it ain't my place to tell him no different. A 'route march' is 'bout as far as to our mailbox at home. Then them city boys get sore feet, so we all ride back in trucks.

Sergeant is kinda like a schoolteacher. He nags some. The captain is kinda like the school board. The majors and colonels, they just ride around and frown, but they don't bother ya none.

This next thing will make Walt and Elmer crack up. I keep gittin' medals for shootin'. Don't know why. The bulls-eye's near as big as a chipmunk head and it don't move. And it ain't shooting back at you, like them Higgett boys back home. All ya gotta do is lay there all comforted like 'n hit it. Ya don't even have to load your own cartridges cuz they come all ready-made in boxes.

Then we have what they call hand-to-hand combat training and git to wrestle with them city boys. Gotta be real careful though, cause they break easy. Ain't like fighting with that 'ole bull back home.

Guess I'm about the best they got in this shootin' and fightin' stuff ... 'cept for ol' Tug Jordan from over in Silver Lake. He joined up same time as me. I'm only 5'6" and 130 pounds, but he's like about 6' 8" and weighs near 300 pounds dry.

Be sure to tell Walt and Elmer to hurry and join before all them other fellers get onto this setup and come stampedin' in here.

Your loving daughter,
Emma Mae

Rejoice! Clean Humor

✦✦✦ First grader proverbs ✦✦✦

A first grade teacher gave her students a list of old proverbs opening lines and asked them to finish each one with how they thought those proverbs might be completed. Their insights are priceless:

1. Don't change horses … until they stop running.
2. Strike while the … bug is close.
3. It's always darkest before … Daylight Saving Time.
4. Never underestimate the power of … termites.
5. You can lead a horse to water but … how?
6. Don't bite the hand that … looks dirty.
7. No news is … impossible.
8. A miss is as good as a … Mr.
9. You can't teach an old dog new … math.
10. If you lie down with dogs, you'll … stink in the morning.
11. Love all, trust … me.
12. The pen is mightier than the … pigs
13. An idle mind is … the best way to relax.
14. Where there's smoke there's … pollution.
15. Happy the bride who … gets all the presents.
16. A penny saved is … not much.
17. Two's company, three's … the Musketeers.
18. Don't put off till tomorrow what … you put on to go to bed.
19. There are none so blind as … Stevie Wonder.
20. Children should be seen and not … spanked or grounded.
21. If at first you don't succeed … get new batteries.
22. When the blind lead the blind … get out of the way.

Don't let your worries
get the best of you.
Just remember,
Moses started out as a basket case.

Share some hearty laughter every day!

✦✦ The difference between men and women ✦✦

A woman's version of responding to a comment about her hair cut:

Woman #1: Oh, you got a haircut ... that's so cute.

Woman #2: Do you think so? I wasn't sure when she gave me the mirror. I mean, you don't think it's too fluffy looking?

Woman #1: Oh my no. No, it's perfect. I'd love to get my hair cut like that, but I think my face is too wide. I'm pretty much stuck with this stuff I think.

Woman #2: Are you serious? I think your face is adorable. And you could easily get one of those layer cuts - that would look so cute on you I think. I was actually going to do that except I was afraid it would accent my long neck.

Woman #1: Oh, I would love to have your neck. Anything to take attention away from this two-by-four I have for a shoulder line.

Woman #2: Are you kidding? I know girls that would love to have your shoulders. Everything drapes so well on you. I mean, look at my arms - see how short they are? If I had your shoulders I could get clothes to fit me so much easier.

Man's version:

Man #1: Haircut?

Man #2: Yeah

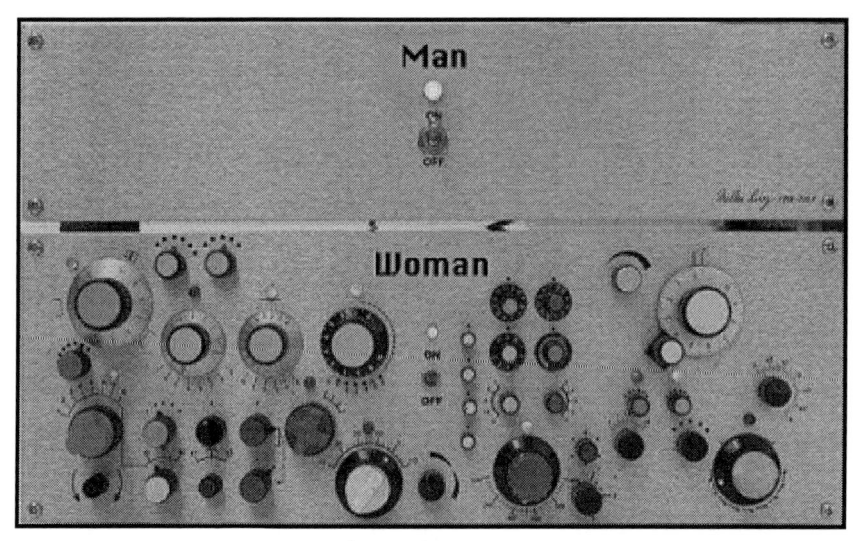

✦✦✦ Creative Signs ✦✦✦

On a maternity room door:
"Push. Push. Push."

At an optometrist's office:
"If you don't see what you're looking for, you've come to the right place."

In a podiatrist's office:
"Time wounds all heels."

Sign over a gynecologist's office:
"Dr. Jones, at your cervix."

On a Plumbers truck:
"We repair what your husband fixed."

Pizza shop slogan:
"7 days without pizza makes one weak."

At a tire shop in Milwaukee:
"Invite us to your next blowout."

On an electrician's truck:
"Let us remove your shorts."

On a taxidermist's window:
"We really know our stuff."

On a Septic Tank Truck sign:
"We're #1 in the #2 business."

Sign on a homeowner's fence:
"Salesmen welcome.
Dog food is expensive."

At the electric company:
"We would be delighted if you send us your payment. However, if you don't, you will be."

Share some hearty laughter every day!

In a veterinarian's waiting room:
"Be back in 5 minutes. Sit. Stay."

At a car dealership:
"The best way to get back on your feet:
miss a car payment."

Outside a muffler shop:
"No appointment necessary.
We can hear you coming."

In a restaurant window:
"Don't stand there and be hungry ...
Come on in and get fed up."

In the front yard of a funeral home:
"Drive carefully.
We'll wait."

In a nonsmoking area:
"If we see smoke, we will assume you are on fire
and take appropriate action."

✦✦ A few thoughts on love and marriage ✦✦

*A man is incomplete until he is married.
After that, he is finished.*

- Dating is a bit like a snowstorm in which you have to suffer through a lot of flakes.

- Love is like an hourglass, with the heart filling up as the brain empties.

- The wise never marry. But if they marry, they become otherwise.

- Marriage is a relationship in which one person is always right and the other is the husband.

- If a wedding is such a great a day for a bride, then why is she marrying a groom instead of the best man?

- Why is it that women always ask questions that apparently have no correct answers?

- Married men tend to forget their mistakes because there is no sense in two people remembering the same things, right?

- A husband once said: I had some words with my wife ... and she had some paragraphs with me.

- So, if at first you don't succeed, why not just try doing it the way your wife told you to do it in the first place.

- Here are two excellent tips for keeping your marriage good:
    1. Whenever you're wrong, admit it.
    2. Whenever you're right, keep your mouth shut.

*Behind every successful man,
there is a surprised woman.*

Share some hearty laughter every day!

✦✦✦ Geography lesson ✦✦✦

You live in Arizona when …
1. You are willing to park 3 blocks away because you found shade.
2. You can open and drive your car
   without touching the car door or the steering wheel.
3. You can attend any function wearing shorts and a tank top.
4. The four seasons are: tolerable, hot, really hot, and stiffling.
5. 'Dry heat' is like what hits you in the face
   when you open the door of an oven heated to 450-degrees.

You Live in California when …
1. You make over $250,000 and still can't afford to buy a house.
3. The fastest part of your commute is going down your driveway.
4. You know how to eat an artichoke.
5. You drive a rented Mercedes to your neighborhood block party.
6. Someone asks you how far away something is and you tell them how long it will take to get there rather than how many miles it is.

You Live in New York City when …
1. You say "the city" and everyone knows you mean Manhattan.
2. You think Central Park is "nature,"
3. You've worn out a car horn.
4. You think eye contact is an act of aggression.

You Live in Maine when …
1. You only have four spices: salt, pepper, ketchup, and Tabasco.
2. Halloween costumes fit over parkas.
3. You have more than one recipe for moose.
4. Sexy lingerie is anything flannel with less than eight buttons.
5. The seasons are: winter, almost winter, and construction.

You Live in the Deep South when …
1. You can rent a movie and buy bait in the same store.
2. "Y'all" is singular and "all y'all" is plural.
3. After living there 5 years, you still hear people say to you, "Y'all ain't from 'round here are ya?"
4. "He needed killin'" is a valid defense.
5. Everyone has two first names, something like:
   Billy Bob, Jim Bob, Mary Sue, Betty Jean, Mary Beth …

Rejoice! Clean Humor

You live in Colorado when …
1. You carry your $3,000 mountain bike atop your $500 car.
2. A pass does not involve a football or dating.
3. The top of your head is bald, but you still have a pony tail.

You live in the Midwest when …
1. You've never met a celebrity, but the mayor knows your name.
2. Your idea of a traffic jam is ten cars waiting to pass a tractor.
3. You have to switch from "heat" to "A/C" on the same day.
4. You end sentences with a preposition: "Where's my coat at?"
5. When asked about your trip to some far away exotic place, you say, "It was different."

You live in The Villages, Florida when ….
1. You eat dinner at 3:15 in the afternoon.
2. All purchases include some kind of coupon, even houses & cars.
3. Everyone can recommend an excellent dermatologist.
4. Road construction never ends anywhere in the state.
5. Cars in front of you seem to be driven by headless people.

✧✧✧ A just reward ✧✧✧

Mildred, the church gossip, and self-appointed monitor of church members' morals, kept sticking her nose into other peoples' business. Other members did not approve of her meddling and gossip, but feared her enough to keep silent.

She made a mistake, however, when she accused George, a new member, of being an alcoholic after she saw his old pickup parked in front of the town's only bar one afternoon.

She told George and several others that everyone seeing it there would know exactly what he was doing. George being a man of few words, just stared at her for a moment and turned and walked away.

George did not explain, defend, or deny. He said nothing.

But later that evening, George quietly parked his pickup in front of Mildred's house … and left it there all night.

Share some hearty laughter every day!

✦✦✦ Georgia on my mind ✦✦✦

A group of Georgia friends went deer hunting and paired off in twos for the day. That night, one of the hunters returned alone, staggering under the weight of an eight-point buck. "Where's Bubba?" the others asked. "Bubba had some kind of a stroke. He's back up the trail a couple of miles," the hunter replied. "You left Bubba laying out there helpless and carried this deer back here instead?" they asked. "Yep, it was a tough call," the hunter said. "But I figured no one is going to steal old Bubba."

A Georgia man came running into the store and said to his buddy, "Bubba, somebody just stole your pickup truck from the parking lot." Bubba replied, "Did you see who it was?" The first man answered, "I couldn't tell, but I wrote down the license number."

Georgia's worst air disaster occurred when a small two-seater Cessna piloted by two native Georgians, crashed into a cemetery. Search and rescue workers have recovered 300 bodies so far and expect the number to climb as digging continues. The pilot and copilot survived the crash and are helping out with recovery efforts.

A Georgia State Trooper pulled over a pickup on the interstate. The trooper asked, "Got any ID?" The driver replied, "Bout whut?"

A Georgia man had a flat tire, so he pulled off to the side of the road and put a bouquet of flowers in front of his car and another behind it. Then he got back in the car to wait. A state trooper showed up and asked the fellow what the problem was. The man replied, "I have a flat tire." The trooper asked, "But what's with the flowers?" The man responded, "When you break down, they always told me to put flares in the front and in the back. I never did understand that either."

---

*After twelve years of therapy
my psychiatrist said something
that brought tears to my eyes.
He said, "No hablo ingles."*

✦✦✦ Really helpful labels ✦✦✦
found on consumer goods

On a Sears hairdryer:
Do not use while sleeping.

On a bag of Fritos:
You could be a winner.
No purchase necessary.
Details inside.

On a bar of Dial soap:
"Directions: Use like regular soap."

Printed on the bottom of Tesco's Tiramisu dessert:
"Do not turn upside down."
(Well duh, a bit late, huh).

On Marks & Spencer Bread Pudding:
"Product will be hot after heating."

On packaging for a Rowenta iron:
"Do not iron clothes on body."
(But wouldn't this save time?)

On Boot's Children Cough Medicine:
"Do not drive a car or operate machinery after taking this medication."

On Nytol Sleep Aid:
"Warning: May cause drowsiness."

On packages of Christmas lights:
"For indoor or outdoor use only."
(As opposed to what?)

On a Japanese food processor:
"Not to be used for the other use."
(And what other use might that be?)

Share some hearty laughter every day!

On Sunsbury's peanuts:
"Warning: contains nuts."
(Talk about a news flash.)

On an American Airlines packet of nuts:
"Instructions: Open packet, eat nuts."
(And is there a step 3?)

On a child's superman costume:
"Wearing of this garment does not enable you to fly."

✦✦✦ Illogical humans ✦✦✦

Why do people go back again and again to look in the refrigerator with the hope that something new to eat will have materialized since the last time they looked? Why do we wash bath towels? Aren't we clean when we use them? If not, then what was the purpose of the bath? And by the way, why is it that no plastic garbage bag will open from the end you try first?

✦✦✦ Doctor and Gun Statistics ✦✦✦
Courtesy of the U.S. Department of Health
and Human Services ... and the F.B.I.

1. The number of physicians in the U.S.: 700,000
2. Accidental deaths caused by Physicians each year: 120,000
3. Accidental deaths per physicians: 0.171

1. The number of gun owners in the U.S.: 80 million
2. The number of accidental gun deaths per year: 1,500
3. The number of accidental deaths per gun owner: 0.0001875

Therefore, statistically speaking, doctors appear to be about 900 times more dangerous than gun owners. This danger is alarming. It would seem that rather than talking about banning guns, perhaps we should be talking about banning doctors. The statistics on lawyers are being withheld out of concern that the shock might cause people to panic and seek medical attention.

Rejoice! Clean Humor

✦✦✦ **Actual newspaper headlines** ✦✦✦

Something Went Wrong in Jet Crash, Expert Says
Police Begin Campaign to Run Down Jaywalkers
Safety Experts Say School Bus Passengers Should Be Belted
Drunk Gets Nine Months in Violin Case
Survivor of Siamese Twins Joins Parents
Farmer Bill Dies in House
Iraqi Head Seeks Arms
Miners Refuse to Work after Death
Stud Tires Out
Prostitutes Appeal to Pope
Panda Mating Fails; Veterinarian Takes Over
Soviet Virgin Lands Short of Goal Again
British Left Waffles on Falkland Islands
Lung Cancer in Women Mushrooms
Eye Drops off Shelf
Teacher Strikes Idle Kids
Squad Helps Dog Bite Victim
Shot Off Woman's Leg Helps Nicklaus to 66
Enraged Cow Injures Farmer with Axe
Plane Too Close to Ground, Crash Probe Told
Juvenile Court to Try Shooting Defendant
Stolen Painting Found by Tree
Two Soviet Ships Collide, One Dies
Two Sisters Reunited after 18 Years in Checkout Counter
Killer Sentenced to Die for Second Time in 10 Years
Never Withhold Herpes Infection from Loved One
Drunken Drivers Paid $1,000 in `84

Share some hearty laughter every day!

War Dims Hope for Peace
If Strike isn't Settled Quickly, It May Last a While
Cold Wave Linked to Temperatures
London Couple Slain; Police Suspect Homicide
Red Tape Holds Up New Bridge
Deer Kill 17,000
Typhoon Rips Through Cemetery; Hundreds Dead
Man Struck by Lightning Faces Battery Charge
New Study of Obesity Looks for Larger Test Group
Astronaut Takes Blame for Gas in Spacecraft
Kids Make Nutritious Snacks
Chef Throws His Heart into Helping Feed Needy
Arson Suspect is Held in Massachusetts Fire
British Union Finds Dwarfs in Short Supply
Ban On Soliciting Dead in Trotwood
Lansing Residents Can Drop Off Trees
Local High School Dropouts Cut in Half
New Vaccine May Contain Rabies
Man Minus Ear Waives Hearing
Deaf College Opens Doors to Hearing
Air Head Fired
Steals Clock, Faces Time
Prosecutor Releases Probe into Undersheriff
Old School Pillars are Replaced by Alumni
Bank Drive-in Window Blocked by Board
Hospitals are Sued by 7 Foot Doctors
Some Pieces of Rock Hudson Sold at Auction
Sex Education Delayed, Teachers Request Training

Rejoice! Clean Humor

✦✦ Anticipated headlines for the year 2035 ✦✦

Ozone created by electric cars now killing millions
in the seventh largest country in the world, California.

White minorities still trying to have English
recognized as California's third language.

Spotted owl plague
threatens Northwestern United States crops and livestock.

Baby conceived naturally
scientists stumped.

Postal service raises price of first class stamp
to $17.89 and reduces mail delivery to Wednesday only.

---

35 year study results:
diet and exercise are the keys to weight loss.

Supreme Court rules that punishment of criminals
violates their civil rights.

Average height of NBA players
is now nine feet, seven inches.

New federal law requires that all nail clippers, fly swatters,
and rolled up newspapers must be registered with the F.B.I.

Congress authorizes direct deposit
of illegal political contributions to campaign accounts.

Average price of a single family home
in Southern California is now $25 million
three bedroom apartments rent for $50,000 a month.

Celebrating Christmas is now officially a felony
as it offends too many people.

IRS sets minimum tax rate at 75%

Share some hearty laughter every day!

✦✦✦ The American Health Care System ✦✦✦

Two patients limp into two different Medical clinics with the same complaint. Both have great difficulty walking and appear to need hip replacement.

The first patient is examined within the hour, is X-rayed the same day and is scheduled for surgery in the following week.

The second patient, after waiting for a week for an appointment, gets in to see his primary care doctor who then refers him to a specialist. After waiting for four and a half months for an appointment with the specialist, patient number two is given an X-ray which he is told will be reviewed within about a month. From the findings, he is then scheduled for surgery six months later.

Why such different treatment for these two patients?
The first is a Golden Retriever. The second is a Senior Citizen.

✦✦✦ Not so well thought-out signs ✦✦✦

Posted on washing machines in a laundromat:
Please remove all your clothes when the light goes out.

In a London department store:
Bargain basement upstairs.

In an office building:
Toilet out of order. Please use floor below.

Notice in health food shop window:
Closed due to illness.

Notice in a farmer's field:
The farmer allows walkers to cross the field for free,
but the bull charges.

On a repair shop door:
We can repair anything.
(Please knock hard on the door as the bell doesn't work.)

✦✦✦ **Obvious -vs- Oblivious** ✦✦✦

A co-worker ask me to help her figure out why she was not able to get her computer to work. In the tangle of wires under her desk, I discovered that she had plugged her computer into a power strip that was plugged back into itself rather than into the wall outlet.

As I was signing for my credit card purchase, the clerk noticed that I had never signed my name on the back of the credit card. She informed me that she couldn't complete the transaction unless that credit card was properly signed on the back. When I asked why, she explained that she was required to compare the signature that I signed on the receipt to the one on the back of the card. So, I signed the back of that credit card in front of her, and she then carefully compared that signature to the one I had just signed on the receipt. As luck would have it, they matched.

I live in a semi-rural area. We recently had a new neighbor call the local township administrative office to request the removal of the Deer Crossing sign on our road. The reason: Too many deer were being hit by cars, and he didn't want them to cross there anymore.

As I was checking for my flight, an airport employee asked me, "Has anyone put anything in your baggage without your knowledge?" I replied, "If it was without my knowledge, how would I know?" He smiled knowingly and nodded, "That's why we ask."

The stop light on the corner near our office buzzes when it's safe to cross the street. As I was crossing the street with a coworker one day, she asked if I knew what that buzzer was for. I explained that it signals for blind people when the light is red. Appalled, she responded, "What on earth are blind people doing driving?"

When my husband and I arrived at an automobile dealership to pick up our car, we were told the keys had been locked in it. We went to the service department and found a mechanic working feverishly to unlock the driver's side door. As I watched from the passenger side, I instinctively tried the door handle and discovered that it was unlocked. "Hey," I announced to the technician, "it's open." And he replied, "Yes, I know ... I already got that side."

Share some hearty laughter every day!

✦✦✦ Peek-a-boo, I see you ✦✦✦

A few years ago, there was an Olympic skier whose actual given name was Picabo Street. Her unusual first name is pronounced Peek-a-boo. Now Miss Street was not only an outstanding athlete, but she was also a nurse who worked in the Intensive Care Unit of a large metropolitan hospital. She was not permitted to answer the telephone there, however, because it caused too much commotion when she would answer the phone saying, "Picabo, I.C.U."

✦✦✦ 20 year anniversary memories ✦✦✦

A woman awoke during the night and noticed that her husband was not in bed. So, she put on her robe and went downstairs to look for him, and found him sitting at the kitchen table with a cup of coffee.

He appeared to be deep in thought, staring at the wall. She watched as he wiped a tear from his eye and took a sip of his coffee.

"What's the matter, dear?" she softly whispered as she stepped into the room. "Why are you down here all alone and looking so forlorn at this time of night?"

The husband looked up and said, "Do you remember 20 years ago when we were dating, and you were only 16?"

His wife replied, "Yes I do." The husband paused ... the words were not coming easily. "Do you remember how your father caught us in the back seat of my car making love?" "Yes, I remember," his wife answered, lowering herself into a chair beside him.

The husband continued. "Do you remember when he shoved that shotgun in my face and said, either you marry my daughter, or I'll send you to jail for 20 years?"

" I remember that too," she replied softly.

The man wiped another tear from his cheek and said, "I would have gotten out today."

Rejoice! Clean Humor

✛✛✛ Doctor notes on medical charts ✛✛✛

The following are actual, unedited, notes, written by doctors on patients' medical charts:

- Patient has chest pain if she lies on her left side for over a year.

- On the second day the knee was better, and on the third day it disappeared completely.

- She has had no rigors or shaking chills, but her husband states she was very hot in bed last night.

- The patient has been depressed ever since she began seeing me ten years ago.

- The patient is tearful and crying constantly. She also appears to be depressed.

- Discharge status: Alive but without permission.

- Healthy appearing, decrepit 69 year-old male, mentally alert but forgetful.

- The patient refused an autopsy.

- The patient has no past history of suicides.

- Patient has left his white blood cells at another hospital.

- Patient's past medical history has been remarkably insignificant, with only a forty pound weight gain in the past three days.

- Patient had waffles for breakfast and anorexia for lunch.

- Patient is numb from her toes down.

- While in the ER, patient was examined, X-rated, and sent home.

- Patient's skin was moist and dry.

Share some hearty laughter every day!

- Occasional, constant, infrequent headaches. *(Say what?)*
- She stated that she had been constipated for most of her life until she got a divorce.
- I saw your patient today, who is still under our car for physical therapy.
- The lab test indicated abnormal lover function.
- The patient was to have a bowel resection. However, he took a job as a stockbroker instead.
- Skin: Somewhat pale but present.
- The pelvic examination will be done later on the floor.
- Patient was seen in consultation by Dr. Thompson, who felt we should sit on the abdomen, and I agree.
- Patient has two teenage children, but no other abnormalities.

The reason people sometimes get lost in thought is because it's unfamiliar territory.

✧✧✧ Country wisdom ✧✧✧

- The best sermons are lived not preached.
- Forgive your enemies. It messes with their heads.
- Life is simpler when you plow around the stumps.
- You can't unsay a cruel thing.
- It don't take a very big person to carry a grudge.
- A bumble bee is faster than a John Deere tractor.
- Words that soak into your ears are whispered, not yelled.
- Most of the stuff people worry about never happens.
- Don't wrestle with pigs. You'll get all muddy and the pigs love it.

✦✦✦ More concise wisdom ✦✦✦

- Blessed are the flexible for they shall not be bent out of shape.
- Never argue with an idiot. People watching may not be able to tell the difference.
- The best way to save face is to keep the lower part shut.
- Light travels faster than sound. And that is why some people appear bright until they open their mouth to speak.
- Middle age is when broadness of mind and narrowness of the waist change places.
- Opportunities always look bigger going than coming.
- Experience is a wonderful thing. It enables you to recognize a mistake when you make it again.
- Learn from the mistakes of others. You can't live long enough to make them all yourself.
- Always read stuff that will make you look good ... in case you die in the middle of it.
- Drive carefully. It is not only automobiles that can be recalled by their maker.
- If you can't be kind, at least have the decency to be vague.
- If you lend someone $20 and never see that person again, it was probably worth it.
- It may be that your sole purpose in life is simply to serve as a warning to others.
- Since it's the early worm that gets eaten by the bird, sleep late.
- And remember, it is the second mouse that gets the cheese.
- When everything's coming your way, you're in the wrong lane.
- Birthdays are good for you. The more you have, the longer you live. Getting older is generally better than the only alternative.
- A truly happy person is one who can enjoy the scenery on a detour.

Share some hearty laughter every day!

✦✦✦ Foreign signs skewering English ✦✦✦

In a Bucharest Hotel Lobby:
"The lift is being fixed for the next day.
During that time you will be unbearable."

In a Leipzig elevator:
"Do not enter the lift backwards and only when lit up."

In a Belgrade elevator:
"To move the cabin, push forward for wishing floor.
If the cabin should enter more persons,
each one should press a number for a wishing floor.
Driving is then going alphabetically by national order."

In a Paris elevator:
"Please leave your values at the front desk."

In a Moscow Hotel:
"You are invited to visit the cemetery
where famous Soviet composers, authors, and artists
are buried daily, except Thursday."

In an Austrian ski hotel:
"Do not perambulate the corridors
in the hours of repose in the boots of ascension."

On a Swiss menu:
"Our wines leave you nothing to hope for."

On a Polish menu:
"Salad of firm's own make,
limpid red beet soup with cheesy dumplings
in the form of a finger, roasted duck let loose,
and beef rashers beaten up
in the country people's fashion."

Japanese detour sign:
"Stop: Drive sideways."
(that would be a great trick)

Share some hearty laughter every day!

On a Japanese air conditioner:
"Cooles and Heates:
If you want just condition of warm in your room,
please control yourself."

In a Tokyo car rental office:
"When passenger of foot heave in sight, tootle horn.
Trumpet him melodiously at first,
but if he still obstacles your passage,
then tootle him with vigour."

In a Hong Kong dress shop:
"Ladies have fits upstairs."

In a Rhodes tailor shop:
"Order your summer suit because it is big rush
we will execute customers in strict rotation."

By a Swedish furrier:
"Fur coats made for ladies from their own skin."

In a Swiss mountain inn:
"Special today - no ice cream."

In a Copenhagen airline office:
"We take your bags and send them in all directions."

In a Budapest zoo:
"Please do not feed the animals.
If you have suitable food, give it to the guard on duty."

In a Norwegian cocktail bar:
"Ladies are requested not to have children in the bar."

In Germany's Black Forest:
"It is strictly forbidden
on our Black Forest camping site
that people of different sex, for instance, men and women,
live together in one tent
unless they are married together for that reason."

Rejoice! Clean Humor

✦✦✦ How to foil junk mailers ✦✦✦

When you get an envelope full of junk advertising material, such as all the inserts in your telephone or utility bill, mail all that garbage back to them with your payment. Let them all throw away their own garbage. Perhaps they will quit sending so much of it to you.

Better yet, when you receive a solicitation with a postage-paid business reply mail envelope included, stuff all that junk mail right back into that postage-paid envelope and mail it back to the junk mail sender so they will have to pay the postage to get it all back.

Or, save up all those postage paid envelopes and then gather up all those annoying door hangers you get from the local pizza places and lawn care folks, and add those to the envelopes you mail back to the junk mail senders. Or, just mail those envelopes back empty if you want to keep them guessing. If we all do this, perhaps eventually, the junk mail senders will quit stuffing our mail boxes with all their garbage. Meanwhile, just have fun with it!

✦✦✦ How to foil telemarketers ✦✦✦

Ask them to talk *verrry slowwwly* because you want to write down every word they say.

Tell the telemarketer you are on "home incarceration" and ask if they could bring you some pizza and some chips.

Cry out in surprise, "Pat. Is that you? Oh my Pat, how have you been?" Hopefully, this will give the caller a few brief moments of pause as she tries to figure out from where you think you know her.

Here are three little words you can use to cut down on nuisance telemarketing calls. Just cheerfully and politely say: "One moment please ..." then put the phone on hold or set it down and go on about your business instead of hanging up. After the phone gives you a beep-beep-beep lost connection signal, hang it up. Just think, if everyone would handle telemarketing calls this way, it might put an end to the telemarketing nuisance.

Share some hearty laughter every day!

When they ask, "How are you today?" Launch into a long story of all the ailments and woes you can think of, for example: "I am so glad that you asked because no one seems to really care these days, and I have so many problems; for instance my arthritis is acting up, my eyelashes are really sore today, and my dog just died ..."

If they say their name and the company name they are calling from, ask them to spell their name and take a lot of time to say each letter very slowly back to them. Then ask them to spell the company name. Then ask them where the company is located. Then ask for their mailing address. Keep asking them personal questions as long as necessary until they give up and hang up.

Tell the telemarketer that you are busy at the moment and ask them if they will give you *their* home phone number so you can call them back later. When the telemarketer explains that they cannot give out their home number, say: "I guess you don't want anyone bothering you at home, right? ... Perhaps you know how I feel, also."

Insist that the caller is really your buddy Leon, playing a joke. "Come on Leon, cut it out. Seriously, Leon, how's your momma?"

Ever get one of those annoying automated phone calls apparently made by a machine with no real person on the other end? This is a telemarketing technique used to determine if numbers are valid and to record the time of day when a person actually answers the phone. Systems like this are also used to document valid phone numbers, including unlisted numbers, and to determine the best time of day for sales people to call. Therefore, to foil this annoying nuisance, whenever you answer a call and no live person responds, press the # button on the phone repeatedly 6 or 7 times. That will cause the machine to report the line as not valid and delete your number.

This will also give you the satisfaction of creating some confusion for those annoying automated dialing systems.

Considering all the lint you get in your dryer,
if you kept drying your clothes
would they eventually just disappear?

Rejoice! Clean Humor

✦✦✦ Hymns for all professions ✦✦✦

The Dentist's Hymn:	Crown Him with Many Crowns
The Weatherman's Hymn:	There Shall Be Showers of Blessings
The Contractor's Hymn:	The Church's One Foundation
The Tailor's Hymn:	Holy, Holy, Holy
The Golfer's Hymn:	There's a Green Hill Far Away
The Politician's Hymn:	Standing on the Promises
The Optometrist's Hymn:	Open My Eyes That I Might See
The IRS Agent's Hymn:	I Surrender All
The Gossip's Hymn:	Pass It On
The Electrician's Hymn:	Send The Light
The Shopper's Hymn:	Sweet By and By
The Realtor's Hymn:	I've Got a Mansion, Over the Hilltop
The Masseur's Hymn:	He Touched Me
The Doctor's Hymn:	The Great Physician

✦✦✦ How to maintain healthy insanity ✦✦✦

- Sit in your parked car with sunglasses on and point a hair dryer out the window at passing cars.

- Page yourself over the intercom and don't disguise your voice.

- Whenever someone asks you to do something for them, ask them if they want fries with that.

- Put your garbage can on your desk and label it "IN"

- Don't use any punctuation (or spaces) in anything you write.

- When you go through a fast food drive-thru, be sure to tell the cashier that your drive-through order is "to go."

- When the money comes out of the ATM, scream, "I Won. I Won. For the third time this week, I won!"

- When leaving the zoo, run to the parking lot, yelling, "Run for your lives, they're loose."

Share some hearty laughter every day!

✦✦✦ Jewish mothers ✦✦✦

There is a big controversy on the Jewish view of when life begins. For many Jewish mothers in the Jewish tradition, the fetus is not considered viable until it graduates from medical school.

Q: Why don't Jewish mothers drink?
A: Alcohol interferes with their suffering.

When the doctor called Mrs. Liebenbaum to tell her that her check came back, she replied, "So did my arthritis."

Q: Why do Jewish mothers make great parole officers?
A: They never let anyone finish a sentence.

A man called his mother and said, "How are you mom?"
His mother replied, "Not so good … I've been very weak."
The son then asked, "Well why are you weak, mom?"
His mother replied, "Because I haven't eaten in 38 days."
The son said, "That's terrible. Why haven't you eaten in 38 days?"
His mother answered, "Because I didn't want my mouth to be filled with food in case you should call."

Q: How many Jewish mothers does it take to change a light bulb?
A: Jewish mothers answer, with a sigh … "Don't bother. I'll just sit in the dark. I don't want to be a nuisance to anybody."

A Jewish boy came home from school and told his mother that he had a part in the school play. She asked, "What part is it?" The boy said, "I play the part of a Jewish husband." The mother scowls and said, "Go back and tell the teacher you want a speaking part."

Q: What's the difference between a Rottweiler and a Jewish mother?
A: Eventually, the Rottweiler lets go.

Did you hear about the bum who walked up to a Jewish mother on the street and said, "Lady I haven't eaten in three days."
"Force yourself," she replied.

Jewish mother sends a telegram:
"Begin worrying. Details to follow."

Rejoice! Clean Humor

✧✧✧ Job application head-scratchers ✧✧✧

"I am extremely loyal to my present firm, so please don't let them know of my immediate availability."

Under qualifications: "I am a man filled with passion, integrity, and can act on short notice. I'm a class act and do not come cheap."

"I intentionally omitted my salary history. I've made money and lost money. I've been rich and I've been poor. I prefer being rich."

"Personal: I am married with nine children, so I do not require prescription drugs.

Note: "Please do not misconstrue my 14 previous jobs as 'job-hopping.' I have never quit a job."

"Marital Status: Often. Children: Various."

"Here are my qualifications for you to overlook."

"I was proud to win the Gregg Typting Award."

✧✧ Reasons given for leaving the last job ✧✧

"Responsibility makes me nervous."

"My previous employer insisted that all employees get to work by 8:45 every morning. I couldn't work under those conditions."

"I met with a string of broken promises and lies, as well as cockroaches."

"I was working for my mom until she decided to move."

"The last company I worked for made me a scapegoat ... just like my three previous employers."

Try to remember: A closed mouth gathers no feet.

Share some hearty laughter every day!

✦✦ Precocious kids one-up their teachers ✦✦

Teacher: John, how do you spell "crocodile?"
John: k-r-o-k-o-d-i-a-l
Teacher: No, John, that is not correct.
John: Well, maybe it's wrong, but you asked me how *I* spell it.

Teacher: What is the chemical formula for water?
Sarah: H I J K L M N O.
Teacher: What in the world are you talking about, Sarah?
Sarah: Well, yesterday you said it's H to O.

Teacher: Willie, name one important thing we have today that we didn't have ten years ago.
Willie: Me.

Teacher: Tommy, why do you always get so dirty?
Tommy: I'm a lot closer to the ground than you are.

(You'll have to be alert, swift, and perceptive to get this one.)
Teacher: Ellen, give me a sentence starting with "I."
Ellen: I is.
Teacher: No, Ellen. Always say, "I am."
Ellen: All right. "I am the ninth letter of the alphabet."

Teacher: "Can anybody give an example of a coincidence?"
Johnny: "My mom and dad got married on the same day at same time."

Teacher: Your composition on "My Dog" is exactly the same as your brother's. Did you copy his?
Desmond: No, teacher. It's the same dog.

Teacher: What do you call a person who keeps on talking when people are no longer interested?
Pupil: A teacher

---

*Today's mighty oak
is just yesterday's nut that held its ground.*

Rejoice! Clean Humor

✦✦✦ Reasons to not mess with a child ✦✦✦

A Kindergarten teacher was observing her classroom of children while they were drawing. As she walked around the room to see each child's work, she came to one little girl who was working very diligently, and she asked what the drawing was. The girl replied, "I'm drawing God." The teacher paused for a moment and then said, "But no one knows what God looks like." Without missing a beat or looking up from her drawing, the little girl replied, "They will in a minute."

A Sunday school teacher was discussing the Ten Commandments with her five and six year olds. After explaining the commandment to "honor thy Father and thy Mother," she asked, "Is there also a commandment that teaches us how to treat our brothers and sisters?" A little boy answered, "Thou shall not kill."

One day a little girl was sitting and watching her mother do the dishes at the kitchen sink when she noticed several strands of white hair on her mother's otherwise brunette head. She asked, "Why are some of your hairs white, mom?" Her mother replied, "Well dear, every time you do something wrong and make me cry or unhappy, one of my hairs turns white." The little girl thought about this for a moment and then said, "So, momma, how come *all* of grandma's hairs are white?"

As the children were in the lunch line in the cafeteria of a Christian elementary school, at the head of the table was a large pile of apples. A teacher had made a note and posted it on the apple tray reading: "Take only ONE. God is watching." Farther down the line, at the other end of the table was a large pile of chocolate chip cookies where a child had placed a note that said: "Take all you want. God is watching the apples."

A prospective father-in-law asked, "Young man, can you support a family?" The surprised groom-to-be replied, "Well, no sir. I was just planning to support your daughter. The rest of you will have to fend for yourselves."

Share some hearty laughter every day!

✦✦✦ The way children see things ✦✦✦

I was driving with my three young children one warm summer evening when a woman in a convertible ahead of us stood up and waved. She was stark naked. As I was reeling from the shock, I heard my 5-year-old shout from the back seat, "Mommy! That lady isn't wearing a seat belt."

A little boy got lost at the YMCA and found himself in the women's locker room. When he was spotted, all the ladies in the room burst into shrieks, grabbing towels and running for cover. The little boy watched in amazement and then asked, "What's the matter? Haven't you ever seen a little boy before?"

A woman was trying to get the ketchup to come out of the ketchup bottle when during her struggle, the telephone rang. So she asked her 4-year-old daughter to answer the phone. The little girl turned around and said, "It's the pastor, mommy." Then she turned back to the phone and said, "Mommy can't come to the phone to talk to you right now because she's hitting the bottle."

While working for an organization that delivers lunches to elderly shut-ins, I used to take my 4-year-old daughter on my afternoon rounds. The various appliances of old age, particularly the canes, walkers and wheelchairs, unfailingly intrigued her. One day I found her staring at a pair of false teeth soaking in a glass. As I braced myself for the inevitable barrage of questions, she quietly whispered to me, "The tooth fairy will never believe this."

A little girl was watching her parents dress for a party. When she saw her dad donning his tuxedo, she warned, "Daddy, you shouldn't wear that suit." "And why not, darling?" "You know that it always gives you a headache the next morning."

A little boy opened the big family Bible and was fascinated as he fingered through the old pages. Suddenly, something fell out of the Bible, and he picked up the object and studied it. What he saw was an old leaf that had been pressed in between the pages. "Mama, look what I found," the boy said. "What have you got there, dear?" With astonishment in his voice, he answered, "I think it's Adam's underwear."

Rejoice! Clean Humor

While walking along the sidewalk in front of his church, a minister heard the intoning of a prayer that nearly made his collar wilt. His 5-year-old son and his playmates had found a dead robin, and thinking that proper burial should be performed, they secured a small box and cotton batting, then dug a hole and made ready for the disposal of the deceased. The minister's son was chosen to say an appropriate prayer, and with sonorous dignity he intoned his version of what he thought his Father always said: "Glory be unto the Faaaather ... and unto the Sonnn ... and into the hole he gooooes."

A little girl had just finished her first week of school. "I'm just wasting my time," she said to her mother. "I can't read, I can't write, and they won't let me talk."

On the first day of school, a child handed his teacher a note from his mother. The note read, "The opinions expressed by this child are not necessarily those of his parents."

✢✢✢ Kids say the funniest things ✢✢✢

One day as a minister was preaching the children's sermon, he reached into his bag of props and pulled out an egg. He pointed at the egg and asked the children, "What's in here?" "I know," a little boy exclaimed. "It's pantyhose."

As the ushers passed around the offering plates, when they came near the little boy's pew, he said in a very loud voice, "Don't pay for me daddy. I'm under five."

The Sunday school teacher asked, "Do you say prayers before eating?" "No sir," Johnny replied, "We don't have to. My mom is a good cook."

After the christening of his baby brother in church, little Johnny sobbed all the way home in the back seat of the car. Several times, his father asked him what was wrong. Finally, the boy replied, "That pastor said he wanted us brought up in a Christian home, but I want to stay with you guys."

Share some hearty laughter every day!

A six-year-old was overheard reciting the Lord's Prayer at a church service: "And forgive us our trash passes, as we forgive those who passed trash against us."

A little boy was attending his first wedding. After the service, his cousin asked him, "How many women can a man marry?" "Sixteen," the boy responded. His cousin was amazed that he had an answer so quickly. "How do you know that?" "Easy," the little boy said. "All you have to do is add it up. Like the preacher said: 4 better, 4 worse, 4 richer, and 4 poorer."

A boy was watching his father, a pastor, write a sermon. "How do you know what to say?" he asked. "Why, God tells me." "Oh. Well then why do you keep crossing things out?"

A little girl became restless as the preacher's sermon dragged on and on. Finally, she leaned over to her mother and whispered, "Mommy, if we give him the money now, will he let us go?"

Terri asked her Sunday School class to draw pictures of their favorite Bible stories. She was puzzled by Kyle's picture, which showed four people on an airplane, so she asked him which story it was meant to represent. He replied that it was a picture of the flight to Egypt. Pointing at each figure, the teacher said, "That must be Mary, Joseph, and baby Jesus. But who's the fourth person?" "Oh, that's Pontius - the pilot."

> *Little Johnny asked his grandma how old she was.*
> *Grandma answered, "39 and holding."*
> *Johnny thought for a moment and then said,*
> *"And how old would you be if you let go?"*

After a service at the Baptist Church, a mother with a fidgety seven-year old boy explained how she finally got her son to sit still and be quiet. About halfway through the sermon, she leaned over and whispered, "If you aren't quiet, the pastor is going to lose his place and he will have to start his sermon all over again." It worked.

Rejoice! Clean Humor

✦✦✦ Letter to a son in boot camp ✦✦✦

Dear son,

I'm writing this slow because I know you can't read fast. We don't live where we did when you left home. Your dad read in the newspaper that most accidents happen within 20 miles of your home, so we moved. I won't be able to send you the address because the last family that lived here took the house numbers when they moved so they wouldn't have to change their address.

But this new place is really nice. It even has a washing machine. I'm not sure about it though. I put a load of clothes in and pulled the chain, and we haven't seen them since.

Auntie Maude sent you a pair of socks she knit. She put a third one in because she heard you have grown another foot since she last saw you.

Now about that coat you wanted me to send. Your Uncle Billy said it would be too heavy to send in the mail with the buttons on, so we cut them off and put them in the pockets.

Jimmy locked his keys in the car yesterday. We were really worried because it took him two hours to get me and your father out.

Your sister had a baby this morning, but I haven't found out what it is yet so I don't know if you are an aunt or uncle. The baby looks just like your brother.

Your Uncle Bobby fell into a moonshine vat last week. Some men tried to pull him out but he fought them off until he drowned. We had him cremated and he burned for three days.

Three of your friends went off a bridge in a pickup truck. Butch was driving. He rolled down the window and swam to safety. Your other two friends were in the back and they drowned because they couldn't get the tailgate down.

Love,
Mom

Share some hearty laughter every day!

✢✢✢ Malapropísms ✢✢✢

Malapropism is a term that describes something spoken or misspoken to a humorous effect. The word first appeared in English around 1660, and was derived from the French phrase mal à propos -- which literally means bad or badly (mal) and appropriate ... thus meaning "ill suited to the purpose." So, the term "malapropism" refers to a humorously misspoken comment. For example:

Someone once described a colleague as "a vast suppository of information"

Here are some more hilarious examples of malapropisms with the words that should have been used in parenthesis:

- Archie Bunker produced a great number of malapropisms that are now classics during the television comedy series All In the Family, including: "vagrant disregard for the law" *(flagrant),* "the Pope is inflammable" *(infallible),* "I've gotta consecrate myself on this newspaper." *(concentrate),* and many more.

- Edith Bunker contributed quite a few also, including her most famous reference to "V.D. Day." *(instead of V-E Day)*

- Mike Tyson gave us: "I might just fade into Bolivian." *(oblivion)*

- Moe of the Three Stooges gave us: "I resemble that remark." *(resent)*

- I think that I can safely say without fear of contraception ... *(contradiction)*

- I am not going to make a skeptical of myself. *(spectacle)*

- Our daughter is just going through phrases. *(phases)*

- He can give you the perpendiculars. *(particulars)*

- He sat there like a big business typhoon. *(tycoon)*

- For all intensive purposes? *(for all intents and purposes)*

Rejoice! Clean Humor

Now you've got the idea, see if you can figure these out:
- Trying to put out the flames with a fire distinguisher.
- That monster is just a pigment of your imagination.
- Isn't that an expensive pendulum round that man's neck?
- Good punctuation means not to be late.
- He's just a wolf in cheap clothing.
- Michelangelo painted the Sixteenth Chapel.
- That guy has extra-century perception.
- "Don't" is a contraption.
- He is the very pineapple of politeness.
- I can't even phantom how that must feel.
- Finally, just try to make sense of this remarkable collection: "If I reprehend anything in this world, it would be the use of my oracular tongue, and a nice derangement of epitaphs."
  (*apprehend, vernacular, arrangement, epithets*)

✦✦✦ Big business mergers ✦✦✦

Big business has seen some huge mergers, such as Exxon/Mobil and AOL/Time Warner. As we contemplate what some future corporate marriages might look like, here are some great possibilities. Just imagine the results if these well known companies merged:

- Hale Business Systems, Mary Kay Cosmetics, Fuller Brush, and W. R. Grace Co. could become: Hale, Mary, Fuller, Grace.

- Polygram Records, Warner Bros., and Zesta Crackers could join forces and become: Poly Warner Cracker.

- 3M could merge with Goodyear and come forth as: MMMGood.

- Zippo Manufacturing, Audi Motors, Dofasco, and Dakota Mining could merge and become: ZipAudiDoDa.

- FedEx could join forces with its major competitor, UPS, and become: FedUP.

- Fairchild Electronics and Honeywell Computers could become: Fairwell Honeychild.

- Knotts Berry Farm and the National Organization of Women could become: Knott NOW.

Share some hearty laughter every day!

✦✦ Important things my mother taught me ✦✦

My mother taught me to appreciate a job well done: "If you're going to kill each other, do it outside -- I just finished cleaning."

My mother taught me religion: "You better pray that will come out of the carpet."

My mother taught me about time travel: "If you don't straighten up, I'm going to knock you into the middle of next week."

My mother taught me logic: "Because I said so, that's why."

My mother taught me foresight: "Be sure you wear clean underwear in case you're in an accident."

My mother taught me irony: "Keep laughing and I'll give you something to cry about."

My mother taught me about osmosis: "Shut your mouth and eat your supper."

My mother taught me about contortionism: "Will you just look at the dirt on the back of your neck."

My mother taught me about stamina: "You will sit there and not move until all that spinach is finished."

My mother taught me about weather: "It looks as if a tornado swept through your room."

My mother taught me how to solve physics problems: "If I yelled because I saw a meteor coming toward you, would you listen then?"

My mother taught me about hypocrisy: "If I've told you once, I've told you a million times ... don't exaggerate ..."

My mother taught me about behavior modification: "Stop acting like your father."

My mother taught me the circle of life: "I brought you into this world, and I can take you out."

Rejoice! Clean Humor

✦✦✦ The Norwegian perspective on life ✦✦✦

Ole is so cheap that after his airplane landed safely he grumbled, "Dere gose fife dollars down da drain fur dat flight insurance."

Lars said: "Ole, stant in front of my car and tell me if da turn signals are verking."
Ole replied: "Yes, No, Yes, No, Yes, No, Yes, No ..."

Ole and Lars went on their very first train ride, and they took along some bananas for lunch. Just as they began to peel them, the train entered a long dark tunnel.
Ole said: "Have you eaten your banana yet?"
Lars relied: "No, not yet."
Ole explained: "Vell, don't touch it den. I yust took vun bite and vent blind."

Scottish scientists recently dug to a depth of 10 meters and were surprised to find traces of copper wire dating back 100 years, leading to the conclusion that their ancestors had built a telephone network more than 100 years ago.

Following this, British scientists dug even deeper and made headlines in UK newspapers that read: "British archaeologists have found traces of copper wire dating more than 200 year old, leading them, to conclude that their ancestors had a high-tech communications network a hundred years earlier than recently reported by the Scots."

Following this, a Minnesota newspaper reported: "After digging deeper than any of the recent archaeological expeditions in the British Isles, a self taught Norwegian archaeologist, Ole Olson, reported that he found absolutely no trace of any copper wire, thus concluding that 300 years ago Norwegians were already using wireless."

Ole said: I haf a big problem.
Lars put a screen saver on my computer for me,
but every time I move da mouse, it disappears.

Share some hearty laughter every day!

Rejoice! Clean Humor

✦✦ Puzzling questions & things to ponder ✦✦

? Is there another word for synonym?

? Since "black box" flight recorders are rarely damaged in a plane crash, why isn't the whole airplane made out of that stuff?

? If a parsley farmer is sued, can they garnish his wages?

? What hair color do they put on driver's licenses of bald men?

? If the police arrest a mime, do they tell him he has the right to remain silent?

? Why do they put braille on drive-through bank machines?

? If people evolved from apes, then why do we still have apes?

? How do they get the deer to cross at that yellow road sign?

? What was the best thing before sliced bread?

? If one synchronized swimmer drowns, do the rest drown too?

? Why is there an expiration date on sour cream?

? If you try to fail and succeed, which have you done?

? If a pronoun is a word used in place of a noun, is a proverb a word used in place of a verb?

? If a pig loses its voice, is it disgruntled?

? Why do croutons come in airtight packages? Aren't they just stale bread?

? Is it good if a vacuum really sucks?

? Why is the third hand on the watch called the second hand?

? If a word is misspelled in the dictionary, how would we know?

? If Webster wrote the first dictionary, where did he find the words?

? Why do we say something is out of whack? What is a whack?

? Why do "slow down" and "slow up" mean the same thing?

? Why do 'tug' boats push their barges?

Share some hearty laughter every day!

- **?** Why do we sing "Take me out to the ball game" when we are already there?
- **?** Why are the seats in a stadium called "stands" when they are made for sitting?
- **?** Why is it called "after dark" when it really is "after light?"
- **?** Doesn't "expecting the unexpected" make the unexpected expected?
- **?** Why do overlook and oversee mean opposite things?
- **?** Why is phonics not spelled the way it sounds?
- **?** If all the world is a stage, where is the audience sitting?
- **?** If love is blind, why is lingerie so popular?
- **?** If you are cross-eyed and have dyslexia, can you read all right?
- **?** Why is bra singular and panties plural?
- **?** Why do we press harder on remote control buttons when we know the batteries are dying?
- **?** Why do we put suits in a garment bag and and all the other garments in a suitcase?
- **?** How come abbreviated is such a long word?
- **?** Why doesn't glue stick to the inside of the bottle?
- **?** Why do banks charge a fee on "insufficient funds" when they know there is not enough money in the account to pay the fee?
- **?** Why does someone believe you when you say there are four billion stars, but check when you say the paint is wet?
- **?** Why did Kamikaze pilots wear helmets?
- **?** Whose bright idea was it to put an "S" in the word "lisp"?
- **?** How do dead bugs get inside enclosed light fixtures?
- **?** If lawyers are disbarred and clergymen defrocked, then why doesn't it follow that electricians can be delighted, musicians denoted, cowboys deranged, models deposed, tree surgeons debarked, and dry cleaners depressed?

✦✦✦ The top 50 oxymorons ✦✦✦

50. Act naturally
49. Found missing
48. Resident alien
47. Advanced BASIC
46. Genuine imitation
45. Airline food
44. Good grief
43. Same difference
42. Almost exactly
41. Government organization
40. Sanitary landfill
39. Alone together
38. Legally drunk
37. Silent scream
36. British fashion
35. Living dead
34. Small crowd
33. Business ethics
32. Soft rock
31. Butt head
30. Military intelligence
29. Software documentation
28. New York culture
27. Extinct life
26. Sweet sorrow
25. Childproof
24. Now, then…
23. Synthetic natural gas
22. Christian scientists
21. Passive aggression
20. Taped live
19. Clearly misunderstood
18. Peace force
17. New classic
16. Temporary tax increase
15. Awfully good
14. Plastic glasses
13. Terribly pleased
12. Computer security
11. Political science
10. Tight slacks
9. Definite maybe
8. Pretty ugly
7. Jumbo shrimp
6. Diet icecream
5. Rap music
4. Working vacation
3. Exact estimate
2. Religious tolerance
1. Microsoft Works

Share some hearty laughter every day!

✦✦✦ Where shall we all gather together? ✦✦✦

A Southern minister delivered a powerful sermon on the evils of alcohol, which he closed with the following emphatic conclusion:

"If I had all the beer in the world, I'd take it and pour it into the river." Then with even greater emphasis he added, "And if I had all the wine in the world, I'd take it and pour it into the river." And finally, he said, "And if I had all the whiskey in the world, I'd take it and pour it into the river."

Then, with a great flourish, he sat down.

Immediately, the song leader stood up and quietly announced: "For our closing hymn, please turn to page number 365 and let us all sing together: 'Shall We Gather at the River'."

✦✦ Performance evaluations - actual quotes ✦✦

"This young lady has delusions of adequacy."

"Sets low personal standards and consistently fails to achieve them."

"Let's just say he's not the sharpest knife in the drawer."

"Has a photographic memory, but the lens cover is glued on."

"This employee is a prime candidate for natural de-selection."

"If you gave him a penny for his thoughts, you would get change."

"If you stand close enough to him, you can hear the ocean."

"Some drink from the fountain of knowledge. He only gargled."

"He has a full six-pack, but lacks the plastic thingy to hold it all together. Since my last report, he has reached rock bottom, and has started to dig even deeper."

Rejoice! Clean Humor

✦✦✦ How to drive in Phoenix, Arizona ✦✦✦

1. Morning rush hour is from 5 AM until noon. Evening rush hour is from noon until 7 PM. Friday's rush hour starts on Thursday morning.

2. The minimum acceptable speed on most freeways is 85 mph. Anything less is considered 'Wussy.'

3. If you actually stop at a yellow light, you *will* be rear ended, cussed out, and possibly shot.

4. Never honk at anyone. Ever. Seriously. That is an offense that can get you shot.

5. Road construction is a permanent and continuous condition in Phoenix. Detour barrels are moved around during the night to make the next day's driving more exciting and entertaining.

6. Watch carefully for road hazards such as drunks, skunks, dogs, barrels, cones, cows, horses, cats, mattresses, shredded tires, squirrels, rabbits, crows, vultures, javelinas, roadrunners, and the coyotes feeding on any and all of these items.

7. If anyone actually has their turn signal on, wave them to the shoulder to let them know it has been accidentally activated. Unless they are retired senior citizens who generally leave their turn signals on permanently.

8. If you are in the left lane and only driving only 70 mpg in a 55 or 65 mph zone, you are considered a road hazard and risk being forcibly run off the road.

9. Forget any traffic rules you have learned elsewhere. Phoenix has its own version of traffic rules. Cars and trucks with the loudest mufflers go first at four-way stops. Trucks with the biggest tires go second. SUV-driving, cell phone-talking moms *always* have the right of way over everyone else.

10. For summer driving, it is highly advisable to wear potholders on your hands.

Share some hearty laughter every day!

✦✦✦ The Pillsbury Doughboy Obituary ✦✦✦

The Pillsbury Doughboy died yesterday of a yeast infection, and complications from repeated pokes in the belly.

Doughboy is survived by his wife, Play Dough, two children, John Dough and Jane Dough, who has a bun in the oven. He is also survived by his elderly father, Pop Tart.

Doughboy was buried in a lightly greased coffin. Many celebrities turned out to pay their respects, including Mrs. Buttersworth, The California Raisins, Betty Crocker, Hostess Twinkies, and Captain Crunch. The grave site was piled high with flours.

Aunt Jemima delivered the eulogy and lovingly described Doughboy as a man who never knew how much he was kneaded. Doughboy rose quickly in show business, but his later life was filled with turnovers. He was not considered a very smart 'cookie' as he wasted much of his dough on half-baked schemes.

Despite being a little flaky at times, he still was considered a roll model for millions.

The funeral was held at 3:50 for about 20 minutes.

✦✦✦ Disciplinary genius ✦✦✦

A school teacher injured his back and had to wear a plaster cast around the upper part of his body. It fit under his shirt and was not noticeable at all.

On the first day of school, with the cast under his shirt, he found himself assigned to the toughest students in school. Nevertheless, walking confidently into the rowdy classroom, he opened the window as wide as possible and busied himself with desk work.

When a strong breeze made his tie flap, he took the desk stapler and stapled the tie to his chest.

Discipline was not a problem from that day forth.

✦✦✦ Politically correct seasons greetings ✦✦✦

Please accept, with no obligation, implied or implicit, my best wishes for an environmentally conscious, socially responsible, low-stress, non-addictive, and gender-neutral celebration of the winter solstice holiday, practiced within the most enjoyable traditions of any or no religious persuasion of your choice or secular practices of your choice, with respect for any and all religious/secular persuasion and/or traditions of others or their choice not to practice religious or secular traditions at all.

I also wish you a fiscally successful, personally fulfilling, and medically uncomplicated recognition of the onset of the generally accepted next calendar year, by whatever calendar system you prefer to use, with all due respect for the calendars of choice of other cultures whose contributions to society have helped to make America great -- but not greater than others of different ethnic preferences.

For this greeting is not to imply that America is necessarily greater than any other country, nor is it the only America in the Western Hemisphere. We extend this greeting without regard to the race, creed, color, age, physical ability, religious faith, or sexual preference of the wishee.

By accepting these greetings, you are also agreeing to accept the following terms. This greeting is subject to clarification or withdrawal. It is freely transferable with no alteration to the original greeting. It implies no promise by the wisher to actually implement any of the wishes for herself or himself or others, and it is void where prohibited by law, and it is also revocable at the sole discretion of the wisher.

This wish is warranted to perform as expected within the usual application of good tidings for a period of one year or until the issuance of a subsequent holiday greeting, whichever comes first. Warranty is limited to replacement of this wish or issuance of a new wish at the sole discretion of the wisher.

Never put both feet in your mouth at the same time or you won't have a leg to stand on.

Share some hearty laughter every day!

✦✦✦ Wise potato counsel ✦✦✦

A girl potato and a boy potato got married, and had a little sweet potato they named Yam. Of course, they wanted the best for Yam, so at the proper time, they told Yam all about the facts of life.

They warned her about going out and getting half-baked, so she wouldn't get into an accident and get mashed or get a bad name for herself like 'Hot Potato' and end up with a bunch of Tater Tots.

Yam said not to worry, no Spud would get her in the sack and make a rotten potato out of her. On the other hand, she wouldn't stay home and be a Couch Potato either. She promised to get plenty of exercise so she would not be skinny like her Shoestring cousins.

When she went off to Europe, Mr. and Mrs. Potato told Yam to watch out for the hard-boiled guys from Ireland and those greasy French fries. And when she went out west, they cautioned her to watch out for the Indians so she wouldn't get scalloped.

Yam promised that she would stay on the straight and narrow and would not associate with those snooty Yukon Golds or guys from the other side of the tracks that advertise 'Frito Lay' on trucks.

Mr. and Mrs. Potato sent Yam to Idaho P.U. *(that's Potato University)* so that when she graduated she'd really be in the potato chips. But in spite of all they did for her, one-day Yam came home and announced that she was going to marry Tom Brokaw.

Tom Brokaw? Mr. and Mrs. Potato were very upset when they heard this. They told Yam she just could not marry Tom Brokaw because after all, he was just … … … a Common Tater.

✦✦✦ Sweet Revenge ✦✦✦

When a three-year-old opened the birthday gift from his grandmother, he found a water pistol and squealed with delight as he headed for the nearest sink. The mother was not very pleased about this, and she turned to her mom and said, "I'm surprised at you. Don't you remember how we used to drive you crazy with water guns?" Grandma just smiled and replied … "Oh yes, I remember."

✦✦✦ Comparing prison and work ✦✦✦

In case you ever get these two environments mixed up, this should make things a little bit clearer.

In prison ... you spend most of your time in a 10x10 cell.
At work ... you spend most of your time in an 8x8 cubicle.

In prison ... you get three meals a day.
At work ... you get a break for one meal and you have to pay for it.

In prison ... you get time off for good behavior.
At work ... you get more work for good behavior.

In prison ... the guards lock and unlock all the doors for you.
At work ... you carry a security card to open all doors for yourself.

In prison ... you can watch TV and play games.
At work ... you could get fired for watching TV and playing games.

In prison ... you get your own toilet.
At work ... you share the toilet with others *(who are often careless)*.

In prison ... they allow your family and friends to visit.
At work ... you aren't supposed to even speak to your family.

In prison ... you spend your life inside bars wanting to get out.
At work ... you spend your time wanting to go to bars.

In prison ... you must deal with sadistic wardens.
At work ... they are called managers.

In prison ... the expenses are all paid by the taxpayers.
At work ... you have to pay all your own expenses to go to work, and they deduct taxes from your salary to pay for prisoner upkeep.

Nevertheless, always look on the bright side about your station in life, whatever it is ... like the optimist who fell from a 30-story building and as he passed each floor on the way down, he yelled out to his friends, "Okay so far ..."

Share some hearty laughter every day!

**Phone out of service?
Give us a call.**

PACIFIC ✻ BELL

Think outside the box.

FOREST LAWN
MEMORIAL GARDENS & MEMORIAL CHAPEL
Pre-Plan Today ·

Rejoice! Clean Humor

✦✦✦ International Pun Contest Winners ✦✦✦

#1. Two vultures boarded an airplane, each carrying two dead raccoons. The stewardess looked at them and said, "I'm sorry, gentlemen, only one carrion allowed per passenger."

#2. Two fish swam into a concrete wall. One turned to the other and said "Dam."

#3. Two Eskimos sitting in a kayak were chilly, so they lit a fire in the craft. Unsurprisingly it sank. Proving once again, that you can't have your kayak and heat it too.

#4. Two hydrogen atoms met. One said "I've lost my electron." The other said "Are you sure?" The first replied "Yes, I'm positive."

#5. Did you hear about the Buddhist who refused Novocain during a root canal? His goal was transcend dental medication.

#6. A group of chess enthusiasts checked into a hotel and were standing in the lobby discussing their recent tournament victories. After about an hour, the manager came out of the office and asked them to disperse. "But, why?" they asked. "Because," he said, "I can't stand chess-nuts boasting in an open foyer."

#7. A woman had twins and gave them up for adoption. One of them went to a family in Egypt and they named him "Ahmal." The other went to a family in Spain and they name him "Juan." Years later, Juan sent a picture of himself to his birth mother. Upon receiving the picture, she told her husband that she wished that she also had a picture of Ahmal. Her husband responded, "Why? They're twins. If you've seen Juan, you've seen Ahmal."

#8. A thief in Paris wanted to steal some paintings from the famous Louvre. After carefully planning, he got past security, stole the paintings, and made it safely to his van. However, he was captured only two blocks away when his van ran out of gas. When asked how he could mastermind such a crime and then make such an obvious error, he replied, "Monsieur, that's the reason I stole the paintings. I had no Monet to buy Degas to make the Van Gogh."

(And you thought we didn't have De Gaulle to tell this one.)

Share some hearty laughter every day!

#9. Mahatma Gandhi walked barefoot most of the time, and that produced an impressive set of calluses on his feet. He also ate very little, which made him rather frail ... and with his odd diet, he suffered from bad breath. All these factors combined to make him ... a super calloused fragile mystic hexed by halitosis.

#10. Then there was the fellow who sent ten different puns to his friends, hoping that at least one of the puns would make them laugh ... but no pun in ten did.

#11. Two antennas met on a roof, fell in love and got married. The ceremony wasn't much, but the reception was excellent.

#12. A jumper cable walked into a bar and the bartender said, "I'll serve you, but just don't try to start anything."

#13. A man walked into a bar with a slab of asphalt under his arm and said: "A beer please, and one for the road."

#14. Two cannibals were eating a clown and one said to the other: "Does this taste funny to you?"

#15. Some friars were behind on their belfry payments so they opened a florist shop to raise some money. Everyone liked to buy flowers from these men of God, but a rival florist across town thought the competition was unfair. So, he asked the good friars to close down their shop. But they refused. He pleaded with them, begging them to close. They ignored him. So, the rival florist hired Hugh MacTaggart, the roughest, most vicious thug in town to "persuade" them to close.

Hugh beat up the friars, totally trashed their store, and told them that he would be back if they didn't close up their shop immediately. Terrified, they finally conceded. Thus once again proving that ... "Only Hugh can prevent florist friars."

Patient: "I can't stop singing 'The Green, Green Grass of Home'."
Doctor: "This sounds like Tom Jones Syndrome."
Patient: "Is this common?"
Doctor: "Well, 'It's Not Unusual'."

Rejoice! Clean Humor

✦✦✦ Frog seeks large bank loan ✦✦✦

A frog went into a bank and approached a bank loan officer. Her nameplate gave her name as Ms. Patricia Whack. "Miss Whack" he says, "I'd like to get a $30,000 loan to take a world cruise."

Patty looked at the frog with questioning eyes and asked his name. The frog said that his name was Kermit Jagger, his dad is Mick Jagger, and that it would be okay because he knew the bank manager. Nevertheless, Patty explained that Kermit would need some collateral in order to get a loan. So Kermit the frog said, "Sure. No problem … I have this …" and he showed Patty a tiny little porcelain elephant about half an inch tall, bright pink, and perfectly formed. Patty was a bit taken back by this, so she said that needed to consult with the bank manager, and she disappeared into a back office.

She told the manager, "There's a frog named Kermit Jagger here who claims to know you and wants to borrow $30,000. And he offered this as collateral *(showing the manager the tiny little pink elephant)*. Then she said, "What in the world is this, anyway?"

Without hesitation, the bank manager said, "It's a Knick Knack, Patty Whack, Give the frog a loan. His old man's a Rolling Stone."

✦✦✦ Once a pun a time ✦✦✦

Aunt Matilda liked Eggs Benedict, but she was afraid to order that dish because she wore dentures and for some reason the hollandaise sauce set up a chemical reaction with the plastic in her dentures to produce a very unpleasant taste in her mouth.

So, she went to her dentist and asked if there was anything that could be done.

"Yes," he said, "we can get a new set of dental plates made for you out of chrome instead of plastic. Chrome will not react adversely to the ingredients in the hollandaise sauce."

"Are you sure this will work?" Aunt Matilda asked.

"Don't worry," the dentist assured her … "There's no plates like chrome for the hollandaise."

Share some hearty laughter every day!

✢✢ A few quarts low on the dipstick of life ✢✢

A lady at work was seen putting a credit card into her computer's floppy drive and pulling it out again very quickly. When I asked her what she was doing, she said that she was shopping on the Internet and they kept asking for a credit card number, so she was trying to use the computer's ATM "thingy."

As a distraught young lady was weeping beside her car, I asked her if she needed some help. She replied, "I knew I should have replaced the battery in this remote control door unlocker. Now I can't get into my car." I asked, "Does your car have an alarm?" She said, "No, just this remote" and she handed it to me, along with her car keys. I took her keys, manually unlocked her door, and said, "Now you can drive to the store to get a new battery."

A while back, we had an intern who was not too swift. One day as she was typing some reports, she turned to a secretary and said, "I'm almost out of typing paper. What do I do?" The secretary replied: "Just use copier machine paper." With that, the intern took her last remaining blank piece of paper, put it on the photocopier and proceeded to make five "blank" copies.

My neighbor works in the operations department in the central office of a large bank. Employees in the field call him when they have computer problems. One night he got a call from a woman in one of the branch banks who said, "I've got smoke coming from the back of my terminal. Are you guys having a fire downtown?"

Police were interrogating a suspect by placing a metal colander on his head and connecting it with wires to a photocopy machine. They wrote, "He's lying" on a piece of paper and put it in the copy machine. Every time they thought the suspect wasn't telling the truth, they pressed the copy button and showed the paper that came out with that message, "He's lying" to the suspect. Believing that the "lie detector" was actually working, the suspect confessed.

A lady was picking through the frozen turkeys at the grocery store but couldn't find one big enough for her family, so she asked a stock boy, "Do these turkeys get any bigger?" The stock boy replied, "No ma'am, they're all dead."

Rejoice! Clean Humor

✦✦✦ Important Recall Notice ✦✦✦

Regardless of model, make, or year, all units known as "human being" will be recalled by the Manufacturer due to a malfunction in the original units that led to the reproduction of the same defect in all subsequent units. This defect is termed, Serious Internal Non-morality or SIN. Some symptoms of this SIN malfunction are:

- a) Loss of direction
- b) Lack of peace and joy
- c) Depression
- d) Foul vocal emissions
- e) Selfishness
- f) Ingratitude
- g) Fearfulness
- h) Rebellion
- i) Jealousy

The Manufacturer offers free, factory authorized repair to correct this SIN defect; and the Repair Technician has offered to bear the entire burden of the entire cost of all repairs. No fee is required.

The number to call for repair is: 800-4PRAYER *(800-477-2937)*

Once connected, please upload and unload the burden of SIN through the REPENTANCE procedure. Then download ATONEMENT from the Repair Technician into the heart component of the human unit. No matter how big or small the SIN defect is, it can and will be replaced with the following:

- a) Love
- b) Joy
- c) Peace
- d) Patience
- e) Gentleness
- f) Goodness
- g) Faith
- h) Meekness
- i) Temperance *(or moderation)*

Please see the operating manual *(www.AV7.org)* for further details.

As an added upgrade, the Manufacturer has made available to all repaired units an enhancement for direct monitoring and ongoing assistance from the Maintenance Technician. Repaired units need only make Him welcome and He will take up permanent residence.

WARNING: Continuing to operate a human unit without this essential correction voids the Manufacturer's warranty and exposes the unit to terrible dangers and problems; and, if not corrected will result in the human unit eventually being incinerated.

Share some hearty laughter every day!

✦✦✦ Letters of Recommendation ✦✦✦

Suggested phrases for those trying to be "politically correct"

For the chronically absent:
    "A man like him is hard to find."
    "It seemed her career was just taking off."

For an employee who drinks to excess:
    "I feel his real talent is wasted here."
    "We generally found him loaded with work to do."
    "Every hour with him was happy hour."

For an employee with no ambition:
    "He could not care less
        about the number of hours he had to put in."
    "You would indeed be fortunate
        to get this person to work for you."

For an employee so unproductive the job is better left unfilled:
    "I can assure you that no person
        would be better for the job."

For an employee not worth considering as a job candidate:
    "I would urge you to waste no time
        in making this candidate an offer of employment."
    "All in all, I cannot say enough good things
        about this candidate or recommend him too highly."

For a stupid employee:
    "There is nothing you can teach a man like him."
    "I most enthusiastically recommend this candidate
        with no qualifications whatsoever."

For a dishonest employee:
    "Her true ability was deceiving."
    "He's an unbelievable worker."

Some minds work like lightning.
A momentary brilliant flash and then all gone.

Rejoice! Clean Humor

✦✦✦ Retarded Grandparents ✦✦✦

After Christmas, a teacher asked her young pupils how they spent their holiday away from school. One child wrote the following:

We always used to spend the holidays with Grandma and Grandpa. They used to live in a big brick house, but when Grandpa got retarded, they moved to Florida. Now they live in a tin box and have rocks painted green to look like grass in their front yard. They ride around on their bicycles and wear name tags because they don't know who they are anymore.

They go to a building called a wrecked center, but they must have got it fixed because it is all okay now, and they do exercises there, but they don't do them very well.

There is a swimming pool too, but in it, they all jump up and down with hats on.

At their gate, there is a doll house with a little old man sitting in it. He watches all day so nobody can escape. But sometimes they sneak out and go cruising in their golf carts.

Nobody there cooks, they just eat out. And they eat the same thing every night -- early birds.

Some of the people can't get out past the man in the doll house. The ones who do get out, bring food back to the wrecked center for pot luck.

My Grandma says that Grandpa worked all his life to earn his retardment and says if I work hard someday I can be retarded too.

When I earn my retardment, I want to be the man in the doll house. Then I will let the people out so they can visit their grandchildren.

A lovely, gracefully aging grandma once said:
I refuse to think of them as chin hairs.
I think of them as stray eyebrows.

Share some hearty laughter every day!

Rejoice! Clean Humor

✦✦✦ S.A.T. Test Answers ✦✦✦

Reportedly collected from tests given to 16-year-old students.

Q: Name the four seasons.
A: Salt, pepper, mustard and vinegar.

Q: Explain one process by which water can be made safe to drink.
A: Flirtation makes water safe to drink because it removes large pollutants like grit, sand, dead sheep, and canoeists.

Q: How is dew formed?
A: The sun shines down on the leaves and makes them perspire.

Q: What is a planet?
A: A body of earth surrounded by sky.

Q: What are steroids?
A: Things for keeping carpets still on the stairs.

Q: What happens to your body as you age?
A: When you get old, your bowels get intercontinental.

Q: What happens to a boy when he reaches puberty?
A: He says good-bye to boyhood and looks forward to adultery.

Q: Name a major disease associated with cigarettes.
A: Premature death.

Q: How can you delay milk turning sour?
A: Keep it in the cow.

Q: What is the Fibula?
A: A small lie.

Q: How are the main parts of the body categorized?
A: The body is consisted into three parts -- the brainium, the borax, and the abdominal cavity. The brainium contains the brain, the borax contains the heart and lungs, and the abdominal cavity contains the five bowels, A, E, I, O, and U.

Share some hearty laughter every day!

Q: What does "varicose" mean?
A: Nearby.

Q: What is the most common form of birth control?
A: Most people prevent contraception by wearing a condominium.

Q: Give the meaning of the term "Caesarian Section."
A: The Caesarian section is a district in Rome.

Q: What is a seizure?
A: A Roman emperor.

Q: What is a terminal illness?
A: When you are sick at the airport.

Q: Give an example of a fungus. What is a characteristic feature?
A: Mushrooms. They always grow in damp places and so they look like umbrellas.

Q: What does the word "benign" mean?
A: Benign is what you will be after you be eight.

Q: What is a turbine?
A: Something an Arab wears on his head.

Q: What is a Hindu?
A: It lays eggs.

✦✦✦ Actual school excuse notes ✦✦✦

These are actual excuse notes written by parents, collected by schools from all over the country (with their original spelling).

- My son is under a doctor's care and should not take P.E. today. Please execute him.

- Please excuse Lisa for being absent. She was sick and I had her shot.

- Dear School: Please exscuse John being absent on Jan. 28, 29, 30, 31, 32, and also 33.

Rejoice! Clean Humor

- Please excuse Roland from P.E. for a few days.
  Yesterday he fell out of a tree and misplaced his hip.

- John was absent because he had two teeth taken out of his face.

- Carlos was absent yesterday because he was playing football and was hurt in the growing part.

- Megan could not come to school today because she has been bothered by very close veins.

- Chris will not be in school cus he has an acre in his side.

- Please excuse Ray from school as he has very loose vowels.

- Please excuse Pedro from being absent yesterday. He had ~~diahre dyrea direathe~~ the runs.

- Please excuse Brenda, she has been sick and under the doctor.

- Irving was absent yesterday because he missed his bust.

- Please excuse Jimmy for being. It was his father's fault.

- I kept Billie home because we had to go Christmas shopping because I don't know what size she wears.

- Sally won't be in school a week from Friday.
  We have to attend her funeral.

- My daughter was absent yesterday because she was tired.
  She spent a weekend with the Marines.

- Please excuse Jason for being absent yesterday.
  He had a cold and could not breed well.

- Please excuse Mary for being absent yesterday.
  She was in bed with gramps.

- Please excuse Jenny for missing school yesterday. We forgot to get the Sunday paper off the porch, and when we found it on Monday, we thought it was Sunday.

Share some hearty laughter every day!

✦✦✦ Sensible advice and observations ✦✦✦

Advice for the day: If you have a lot of tension and you get a headache, do what it says on the aspirin bottle: "Take two aspirin" and "Keep away from children."

When I die, I want to die like my grandfather who died peacefully in his sleep. Not screaming like all the passengers in his car.

The problem with the designated driver program, is that it is not a desirable job; but if you ever get sucked into doing it, have fun with it. At the end of the night, drop them off at the wrong house."
--Jeff Foxworthy

If a woman has to choose between catching a fly ball and saving an infant's life, she will choose to save the infant's life without even considering if there is a man on base. --Dave Barry

Relationships are hard. It's like a full time job, and we should treat it like one. If your boyfriend or girlfriend wants to leave you, they should give you two weeks' notice, there should be severance pay, and they should have to find you a temp.

Remember in elementary school, you were told that in case of fire you have to line up quietly in a single file line from smallest to tallest. What is the logic in that? Do tall people burn slower?

Suppose you were an idiot. And suppose you were a member of Congress ... but I repeat myself. --Mark Twain

You can say any foolish thing to a dog, and the dog will give you a look that says, 'My God, you're right. I never would've thought of that.' --Dave Barry

If you have ever wondered about the common sense of people who spend $2.00 for a bottle of Evian water, just spell Evian backwards and you will understand what makes them do it. naive

People seem to read the Bible a whole lot more as they get older. Perhaps because they are cramming for the final exam.

✦✦✦ Whatever Comes To Mind ✦✦✦

A minister decided to do something a little different one Sunday morning. He said "Today, I am going to say a single word and you are going to help me preach. Whatever single word I say, I want you to sing whatever hymn comes to your mind.

The pastor shouted out "Cross." Immediately, the congregation started singing in unison "The Old Rugged Cross."

The pastor hollered out "Grace." Without hesitation, the congregation began singing "Amazing Grace, how sweet the sound."

The pastor said "Power." Again, without hesitation, the congregation sang "There is power in the blood …"

Then the pastor said "Sex" and the congregation fell into shocked silence. They all look around at each other, afraid to say anything.

But then, from the back of the church, a little 87 year old great-grandmother stood up and began to sing, "Precious Memories."

✦✦✦ Smart Answers ✦✦✦

When it was mealtime, a flight attendant ask a passenger, "Would you like dinner?" The passenger responded, "What are my choices?" The attendant replied: "Yes or no."

A cop stopped a car for speeding. The kid who was driving rolled down his window. The cop said, "I've been waiting for you all day." The kid replied, "Yeah, well I got here as fast as I could." When the cop finally stopped laughing, he sent the kid on his way without a ticket.

A truck was rolling down the freeway when a sign appeared that read, "Low Bridge ahead." The bridge came up too quickly for the truck to stop and it got stuck under the bridge. Cars began to back up for miles. Finally, a patrol car arrived and the officer came up to the truck driver and said, "Stuck, huh?" The driver said, "No sir, I was delivering this bridge and ran out of gas."

Share some hearty laughter every day!

✦✦✦ Brilliant crooks and criminal actions ✦✦✦

During a holdup in Long Beach, California, when the would-be robber's 38-caliber revolver failed to fire at his intended victim, the robber did something that can only inspire wonder. He peered down the barrel and tried the trigger again. This time it worked.

After stopping for drinks at a bar, a bus driver in Zimbabwe discovered that the 20 mental patients he was supposed to be transporting had escaped. Not wanting to admit his incompetence, the driver went to a nearby bus stop and offered everyone waiting there a free ride. He then delivered the passengers to the mental hospital, telling the staff that the patients were very excitable and prone to bizarre fantasies. His deception wasn't discovered for three days.

A man walked into a Circle-K, put a $20 bill on the counter, and asked for change. When the clerk opened the cash drawer, the man pulled a gun and demanded all the cash in the register. The clerk promptly gave it all to him. The would-be robber took the cash and fled, leaving his $20.00 bill on the counter. The total amount of cash he got from the drawer was $15.43. Which begs the question: If someone points a gun at you and gives you more money than he takes, has a crime been committed?

A guy wanted some booze really bad but he had no money. So, he decided that he would throw a cinderblock through a liquor store window, grab some liquor, and run. He lifted up this big cinderblock and heaved it over his head at the window. But the liquor store window was made of Plexiglas, so the cinderblock bounced back and hit the would-be thief on the head, knocking him unconscious. The whole event was caught on a security videotape. I guess you could call this instant justice.

As a female shopper exited a New York convenience store, a man grabbed her purse and ran. The clerk immediately called 911, and the woman was able to give the police a detailed description of the purse snatcher. Within minutes, the police apprehended the thief, put him in the squad car, and drove back to the store. When they took him out of the car and told him to stand there for a positive ID, this brilliant thief pointed to the victim and said, "Yes, officer, that's her. That's the lady I stole the purse from."

Rejoice! Clean Humor

The Ann Arbor News crime column reported that a man walked into a Burger King in Ypsilanti, Michigan, at 5 AM, flashed a gun, and demanded cash. The clerk said he couldn't open the cash register without a food order, so would-be thief ordered onion rings. But then the clerk said that onion rings weren't available for breakfast, so the frustrated thief, just gave up and walked away.

> *If at first you don't succeed,*
> *don't ever take up sky diving.*

✦✦✦ As the memory begins to fade ✦✦✦

Two elderly ladies had been friends for many decades and had shared all kinds of activities and adventures together. But in recent years, their activities had been limited to meeting a few times a week to play cards.

One day as they were playing cards, one of them looked at the other and said, "Now don't get mad at me. I know we've been friends for a long time ... but I can't remember your name right now. I've thought and thought, but I just can't remember it. Please tell me again what your name is." Her friend glared at her for a few minutes and finally said, "How soon do you need to know?

Three sisters, ages 92, 94, and 96 lived together in the same house. One night the 96 year old drew a bath, put one foot in, and then stopped with a puzzled look on her face. After a minute pause, she yelled downstairs and asked, "Was I getting into or out of the bath?" Her younger sister (the 94-year-old) yelled back, "I don't know. I'll come up and see." She started up the stairs ... but then paused half-way up and yelled out, "Was I going up the stairs or down?"

The youngest sister (the 92 year old) was sitting at the kitchen table having a cup of tea and listening to her sisters. She just shook her head and said, "I sure hope I never get that forgetful" ... and she knocked on wood for good measure. Then she yelled up to them, "I'll come and help you both ... as soon as I see who's at the door."

Share some hearty laughter every day!

✣✣ What your computer is trying to tell you ✣✣

It says: "Cannot read from drive D:"
It means: "Put the CD in right side up."

It says: "Not enough memory"
It means: "I don't care how much you've got, it's not enough."

It says: "Installing program to C:\...."
It means: "I will be writing some files into the c:\windows folder and some into the c:\windows\system folder where you will *never* find them ... *in part, that is because they will have names that correspond to no known programs ever published.*"

It says: "Please Wait...."
It means: "Indefinitely."

It says: "Press Any Key"
It means: "Press any key you like, but I'm not moving."

It says: "Please insert disk 5"
It means: "Because I know darn well there are only 4 disks."

It says: "Directory does not exist."
It means: "Oops. Not any more it doesn't."

It says: "The application caused an error. Choose Ignore or Close."
It means: "It makes no difference to me what you choose, you are never getting your work back."

It says: "Fatal Error #1A4-254651230E contact technical support."
It means: "... you will be kept on hold for 30 minutes, and then told that it is a hardware problem."

```
Warning                                          ☒
         Broken window. Watch out
            for glass fragments.
    ⚠    Operating system overwritten.
         Please reinstall all your software.

                  [  OK  ]
```

✢✢✢ To believe or not believe? ✢✢✢

Once upon a time, an atheist walked through some woods in Alaska, admiring all that evolution had created. He said to himself: "What majestic trees. What a powerful river. What amazing animals."

Then he heard a rustling in the bushes behind him, and as he turned to look, he saw a Kodiak bear standing up about 13-feet tall and about to charge toward him.

So he took off running as fast as he could … but glancing over his shoulder, he could see that the bear was rapidly closing on him.

With tears streaming down his face, he somehow ran even faster … but as he looked back he could see that this huge bear was even closer. His heart pounded in his chest as he tried to run faster still … but alas, he tripped and fell to the ground and the bear was then directly over him with it's huge paw about to strike him. In shear panic, the atheist yelled out: *"Oh my God."*

Instantly, time froze. The bear also froze in time. The forest became stone silent. Even the river stopped moving. A brilliant light shone down from above and a thunderous voice exploded as God spoke:

"You have denied my existence all these years.
"You have taught others that I don't exist.
"And you have credited my creation to some cosmic accident.
"Do you now expect me to help you out of this predicament?
"Are you now a believer in me?"

The atheist looked up toward the light and said, "Oy vey, it would be hypocritical of me to confess to being a believer now after all these years, but could you perhaps make the bear a Christian?"

Very well, God said.

The light went off. The river resumed running. The sounds of the forest returned … and the bear dropped down on his knees, brought both paws together, bowed his head and said: "Lord, thank you for this food that I am about to receive. Amen."

Share some hearty laughter every day!

✛✛✛ Keeping God out of public schools ✛✛✛

92 students filed into a crowded auditorium with their traditional graduation caps and rich maroon gowns flowing. Dads swallowed hard behind broad smiles and moms brushed away tears of joy.

But the class would not be allowed to pray at this commencement because of the court ruling prohibiting prayer in public schools. The principal and several students were careful to stay within the stipulated guidelines. They gave inspiring and challenging speeches, but no one dared to mention divine guidance. The speeches were nice, but mostly routine ... until the final speech.

The last student to speak walked to the microphone and stood still and silent for a moment looking out over the crowd. And then it happened. All 92 students ... in unison ... suddenly sneezed.

The student on stage smiled broadly as he gazed out at the audience and said, "God bless you, each and every one of you" and then walked off stage.

The audience jumped to their feet and exploded in applause.

In spite of the court ruling that took away the student's right of free speech, this graduating class found a unique way to invoke God's blessing on their future ... with or without court approval.

In God We Trust and United We Stand.

✛✛✛ A toast for friends and family ✛✛✛

Here's to friends both near and far.
Here's to woman, man's guiding star.
Here's to friends we've yet to meet.
Here's to those here: all here I greet.
Here's to childhood, youth, old age.
Here's to prophet, bard, and sage.
Here's to health for every one.
Peace on earth, and heaven won.

May your troubles be less, your blessings more,
and may nothing but happiness, come through your door.

Rejoice! Clean Humor

✦✦✦ Did you know? ✦✦✦

- 111,111,111 x 111,111,111 = 12,345,678,987,654,321

- The average number of people in airplanes flying over the U.S. any given hour is 61,000.

- If you count by spelling out all the numbers, you have to count to one-thousand to get to the first occurrence of the letter "A."

- Half of all Americans live within 50 miles of their birthplace

- Bulletproof vests, fire escapes, windshield wipers, and laser printers were all invented by women.

- The only food that never spoils is honey.

- Only 28% of Africa is wilderness, but 38% of North America is wilderness.

- Intelligent people have more zinc and copper in their hair.

- The world's youngest parents were age 8 and 9 and lived in China in 1910.

- The first novel ever written on a typewriter was Tom Sawyer.

- San Francisco's famous cable cars are the only *mobile* National Monuments.

- If a statue in the park of a person on a horse has both front legs in the air, that person died in battle. If the horse has one front leg in the air, that person died as a result of wounds received in battle. If the horse has all four legs on the ground, that person died of natural causes.

- In Shakespeare's time, mattresses were secured on bed frames by ropes. Pull on the ropes to tighten the mattress and make the bed firmer. Hence the phrase, "Goodnight, sleep tight."

How come we never hear any father-in-law jokes?

Share some hearty laughter every day!

✦✦✦ The most versatile two-letter word ✦✦✦

"Up" has more meanings than any other two-letter word. Perhaps more meanings than any other word, period.

Why is it that in the morning we wake *up*?

And why does a topic for discussion come *up*?

Why do we speak *up*? Why are people *up* for election? Why is it *up* to a secretary to write *up* a report? Why do we call *up* our friends? Why do we brighten *up* a room, polish *up* the silver, warm *up* leftovers, clean *up* the kitchen, lock *up* the house, fix *up* an old car, or fix *up* the house?

Why do people stir *up* trouble, line *up* for tickets, work *up* an appetite, and think *up* excuses?

And why is it so special to be dressed *up*?

Sometimes this word *up* can be very confusing:

A drain must be opened *up* when it gets stopped *up*. How can one open *up* a store in the morning and then close it *up* at night?

We seem to be pretty mixed *up* about *up*.

To be knowledgeable about the proper uses of *up*, look *up* the word *up* in the dictionary. In a desk-sized dictionary, it takes *up* almost 1/4th of the page and has *up* to thirty definitions.

If you are *up* to it, you might try building *up* a list of the many ways *up* is used. It will take *up* a lot of your time, but if you don't give *up*, you may wind *up* with a hundred or more.

When it threatens to rain, we say it is clouding *up*. But then when the sun comes out, we say it is clearing *up*, and when it doesn't rain for a while, we say things dry *up*. We could go on and on with more examples of the word *up* in which it sometimes seems to contradict itself. But perhaps we should now wrap this *up*, because our time is *up* ... so, I guess it is now time to shut *up*.

Rejoice! Clean Humor

✦✦✦ Website name mistakes ✦✦✦

To operate a business in today's world you need a website and a good domain name. But be very careful when considering the name you choose or you could end up with problems. Look closely:

- A site that was intended to be known as 'Who Represents' where one can find the name of the agent who represents a celebrity, ended up with this problem: www.whorepresents.com

- Experts Exchange, a knowledge base where programmers can exchange advice became: www.expertsexchange.com

- Therapist Finder became: www.therapistfinder.com

- In New South Wales, the Mole Station Nursery became: www.molestationnursery.com

- Looking for an Internet Service Provider, commonly known as an "I.P." became: www.ipanywhere.com

These few listed here are not the worst problems that have turned up. Some others are too bad to be printed in this "G" rated book.

✦ Long sought answers to crucial questions ✦

1. How do you catch a unique rabbit? -- Unique up on it.
2. How do you catch a tame rabbit? -- Tame way, unique up on it.
3. How do crazy people go through the forest? On the psycho path.
4. How do you Get Holy Water? -- You boil the hell out of it.
5. What do fish say when they hit a concrete wall? -- Dam.
6. What do Eskimos get from sitting on the ice too long? -- Polaroid's
7. What do you call a boomerang that doesn't work? -- A stick.
8. What do you call cheese that isn't yours? -- Nacho cheese.
9. What do you call Santa's helpers? -- Subordinate clauses.
10. What lies at the bottom of the ocean twitching? A nervous wreck.
11. What kind of coffee was served on the Titanic? -- Sanka.
12. What's the difference between a bad golfer and a bad skydiver?
    A bad golfer goes, "Whack, dang."
    A bad skydiver goes, "Dang, Whack."

Share some hearty laughter every day!

✦✦ You have to try to laugh at all the taxes ✦✦
(because the situation is so ridiculous)

Here is a *partial* list of taxes that are currently imposed on us:

Accounts Receivable Tax	Building Permit Tax
Capital Gains Tax	CDL license Tax
Cigarette Tax	Corporate Income Tax
Dog License Tax	Federal Income Tax
Federal Unemployment Tax	Fishing License Tax
Food License Tax	Fuel permit tax
Gasoline Tax	Hunting License Tax
Inheritance Tax	Inventory Tax
Liquor Tax	Local Income Tax
Luxury Tax	Marriage License Tax
Medicare Tax	Property Tax
Real Estate Tax	Septic Permit Tax
Service charge taxes	Social Security Tax
Road usage taxes (truckers)	Sales Tax
Recreational Vehicle Tax	Road Toll Booth Tax
School Tax	State Income Tax

State Unemployment Tax (SUTA)
  Telephone federal excise tax
  Telephone federal universal service fee tax
  Telephone federal, state and local surcharge taxes
  Telephone minimum usage surcharge tax
  Telephone recurring and non-recurring charges tax
  Telephone state and local tax
  Telephone usage charge tax

Toll Bridge Taxes	Toll Tunnel Taxes
Traffic Fines (indirect taxation)	Trailer Registration Tax
Utility Taxes	Vehicle Registration Tax
Vehicle Sales Tax	Watercraft Registration Tax
Well Permit Tax	Workers Compensation Tax

And just think ... not one of these taxes existed 100 years ago, our nation was the most prosperous in the world, we had no national debt, we had the largest middle class in the world, and moms were able to stay home to raise the kids. What happened?

✦✦✦ Practical Definitions ✦✦✦

Arbitrator: A cook that leaves Arby's to work at McDonalds.
Avoidable: What a bullfighter tried to do.
Bernadette: The act of torching a mortgage.
Burglarize: What a crook sees with.
Counterfeiters: Workers who put together kitchen cabinets.
Eclipse: What a barber does for a living.
Eyedropper: A clumsy ophthalmologist.
Heroes: What a guy in a boat does.
Leftbank: What the robber did with his bag full of money.
Misty: How golfers create divots.
Paradox: Two physicians.
Parasites: What you see from the top of the Eiffel Tower.
Pharmacist: A helper on the farm.
Polarize: What penguins see with.
Primate: Removing your spouse from in front of the TV.
Relief: What trees do in the Spring.
Rubberneck: What you do to relax your wife.
Selfish: What the owner of a seafood store does.
Sudafed: Litigation brought against a government official.

✦✦✦ Dictionary for Women ✦✦✦

Argument: A discussion that occurs when a wife is right, but the husband has not yet realized that.
Cantaloupe: Gotta get married in a church.
Clothes dryer: An appliance designed to eat socks.
Diet soda: A drink you buy at a convenience store to go with a large bag of potato chips.
Eternity: The last two minutes of a football game.
Exercise: To walk up and down a mall, occasionally stopping to make a purchase.
Grocery list: What you spend a half an hour writing, then forget to take to the store.
Hair Dresser: Someone who is able to create a style that you will never be able to duplicate.
Patience: The most important ingredient for dating, marriage, and children.

Share some hearty laughter every day!

✦✦✦ It's great to be a man ✦✦✦

- You can open all your own jars.
- Wrinkles add character.
- Wedding Dress $5,000. Tux rental $100.
- One mood all the time.
- Phone conversations are over in 30 seconds flat.
- A five-day vacation requires only one suitcase.
- You get extra credit for the slightest act of thoughtfulness.
- If someone forgets to invite you to something, you can still be friends.
- Your underwear is only $8.95 for a three-pack.
- If another guy shows up at the party in the same outfit, you might become lifelong friends.
- You don't need to know the names of more than five colors.
- The same hairstyle lasts for years, maybe decades.
- You don't have to shave below your neck.
- One wallet and one pair of shoes, all one color, for all seasons.
- You can do your nails with a pocketknife.
- Christmas shopping takes only 45 minutes on December 24th.

✦✦✦ CEO Power ✦✦✦

Feeling it was time for a shakeup, a company board of directors hired a new CEO. Determined to rid the company of any slackers, on his first day on the job, the new CEO took a tour of the company's offices to see what he might find. In one room full of employees, the new CEO noticed a young fellow leaning against a wall. So, wanting to let all of the employees know that he meant business, the new CEO walked up to him and asked, "And how much money do you make a week?" A little surprised, the young fellow looked up at him and said, "Well, I make about $300.00 a week, why?"

The CEO handed the young fellow $1,200 in cash and screamed, "Here's four weeks pay; now get out and don't come back. Feeling pretty good about his first very firing, the CEO looked around the room and said, "Does anyone want to tell me what that goof-off did here?" A sheepish voice from the back of the room said, "That was the pizza delivery guy from Domino's."

Rejoice! Clean Humor

✦✦ Fascinating facts about the year 1904 ✦✦

The average life expectancy in the U.S. was 47 years.
Only 14% of the homes in the U.S. had a bathtub.
Only 8% of the homes had a telephone.
A 3-minute call from Denver to New York City cost $11.00.

There were only 8,000 cars in the entire country, only 144 miles of paved roads, and maximum speed limit in most cities was 10 mph.

Alabama, Mississippi, Iowa, and Tennessee were each more heavily populated than California. With 1.4 million residents, California was only the 21st most populated state in the Union. And the population of Las Vegas, Nevada was 30 people.

The average wage in the U.S. was 22 cents an hour.
The average U.S. worker earned between $200 and $400 per year.

A good accountant might earn $2,000 per year, a dentist $2,500, a veterinarian between $1,500 and $4,000, and a mechanical engineer about $5,000 per year.

More than 95% of all births took place at home.
90% of all physicians had no college education. Instead, they just went to special medical schools, many of which were condemned by the government as "substandard."

Sugar cost 4-cents a pound. Eggs were 14-cents a dozen. Coffee was 15-cents a pound.

Most women washed their hair only once a month, and used borax or egg yolks for shampoo.

The five leading causes of death in the U.S. were:
1. Pneumonia and influenza
2. Tuberculosis
3. Diarrhea
4. Heart disease
5. Stroke

The American flag had 45 stars. Arizona, Oklahoma, New Mexico, Hawaii, and Alaska had not yet been admitted to the Union.

Share some hearty laughter every day!

There was no Mother's Day or Father's Day.
Two of every 10 U.S. adults could not read or write.
Only 6% of all Americans had graduated from high school.

Marijuana, heroin, and morphine were all legally available over the counter at corner drugstores. One pharmacist advertised, "Heroin clears the complexion, gives buoyancy to the mind, regulates the stomach and bowels, and is a perfect guardian of health."

There were only 230 reported murders in the entire U.S.

Try to imagine what it may be like in another 100 years.

✦✦ Tell-tale signs of 21st century progress? ✦✦

- You get up in the morning and go online to check your email and the news before even getting your coffee.

- You e-mail the person who works at the desk right next to you.

- Your excuse for not staying in touch with friends and family is that you don't have current e-mail addresses for them.

- Almost all commercials on TV include a web site address.

- You have a list of 15 different telephone numbers to reach your family of three.

- You pull up in your own driveway and use your cell phone to see if anyone is home to help you carry in the groceries.

- Leaving the house without your cell phone *(which you didn't even have for the first 20, 30, or 60 years of your life)*, is now a cause for panic ... and you have to go back to get it ... because now, you just can't leave home without it.

I know you think you understand what you thought you heard me say, but I'm not sure you realize that what you thought you heard me say is not what I really meant.

✦✦✦ Insightful Wisdom ✦✦✦

Opportunity may knock once,
but temptation bangs on your front door forever.

Some minds are like concrete …
thoroughly mixed up and permanently set.

Many folks want to serve God,
but only as advisors.

We were called to be witnesses,
not lawyers or judges.

Don't put a question mark
where God put a period.

Don't wait for six strong men
to take you to church.

Forbidden fruits create many jams.

God doesn't call the qualified.
He qualifies the called.

God grades on the cross, not the curve.

God promises a safe landing,
not a calm passage.

If God is your co-pilot, swap seats.

Don't give God instructions.
Just report for duty.

If we truly trust in God,
the task ahead of us is never as great
as the Power behind us.

✦✦✦✦✦✦✦

Share some hearty laughter every day!

✦✦✦ Index ✦✦✦

Introduction: Laughing is good exercise . . .	1
How to survive life's BMUPs in the road . .	3
Many reasons why laughter is good for you .	4
How to clean a cat	6
Genius Thieves	7
Bank Robbery 101	7
Backyard Archaeologist	8
Early warning phone call	10
Beware of tall dark strangers	10
I can hear you just fine	11
What red lights?	12
A perfectly logical explanation	12
And you think you had a bad day	13
Some bumper stickers make a good point . .	14
Hilarious quotes from the rich and famous .	16
Impressive Funeral	18
Kaput tombstone	18
Chinese Proverbs	18
The AAADD Syndrome	19
Interview Slam Sunk	20
Accident Claim Explanations	20
Some golfers are remarkably thoughtful . . .	22
Airline Maintenance Solutions	22
Airline Cabin Announcements	24
Just send in the Marines	26
Read the Bible readerboard	26
The Art of Direct and Cross Examination . .	27
Baptismal service down by the river	31
Eloquent prayer ... prompts a question . . .	31
Born a Baptist ... but now?	32
Shouting Oh God! readerboard	32
The Middle Wife	33
Trying to grade papers with a straight face .	34
Daffynitions	36
Very punny	37
"Dumb" ... like a fox	38

Share some hearty laughter every day!

She was sooooo blonde	39
Stay! Stay! Do you hear me?	40
Flying coach or first class?	40
Snooty cat with bouffant hairdo	41
To catch a thief	42
Blonde handy-woman	42
Blonde officer stops blonde speeder	43
Small pink curtains	43
Progressive parenting	44
How to avoid losing your mind	45
Blonde helicopter pilot	46
Blonde stewardess gets stuck in her room	47
Wonderful new inventions by blondes	47
Blonde resurrects dead rabbit	48
Blonde co-ed takes final exam	49
Illiterate Write for Free Help billboard	49
Creative answering machine messages	50
Epitaphs	54
Cemetery End of the Road	54
Church bulletin bloopers	56
Don't let worries kill you readerboard	56
From the school of higher learning	57
Choice excerpts from actual exam papers	60
As easy as swatting flies	61
Burma Shave Signs	62
Can you hear me now?	64
So ... what foods are safe to eat?	65
fi yuo cna raed tihs	65
Classic classified ads	66
A woman's revenge	68
Pastoral visit	68
Who's afraid ofa little old ride like that?	69
Clever translations	70
How well does cold water clean?	71
Actual tech-support calls	72
Murphy's laws of computing	73
Give me back my dog	74
Do not enter -- Entrance Only	75
Disorder in the court	76

Marriage seminar	77
No nursing home in my future	78
Answers from traffic school exams	79
Think a gallon of gas is expensive?	79
Logical answers to key health questions	80
Doctor tales	81
Safe driver awards	82
Did you ever wonder why?	82
Small cow carrier & Police car in cement	83
Deep philosophical questions to ponder	84
Notes children wrote to their pastors	86
English is a crazy, illogical language	87
Letter home from Marine boot camp	88
First grader proverbs	90
The difference between men and women	91
Man single switch -vs- woman's switch panel	91
Creative signs	92
No smoking bus exhaust	93
A few thoughts on love and marriage	94
Geography lesson	95
A just reward	96
Georgia on my mind	97
Really helpful labels on consumer goods	98
Illogical humans	99
Doctor and Gun Statistics	99
Actual newspaper headlines	100
Anticipated headlines for the year 2035	102
The American Health Care System	103
Not so well thought-out signs	103
Obvious -vs- Oblivious	104
Peek-a-boo, I see you	105
20 year anniversary memories	105
Doctor notes on medical charts	106
Country wisdom	107
Very concise wisdom	108
Serious speed law enforcement	109
Foreign signs skewering English	110
How to foil junk mailers	112
How to foil telemarketers	112

Share some hearty laughter every day!

Hymns for all professions	114
How to maintain healthy insanity	114
Jewish mothers	115
Job application head-scratchers	116
Reasons given for leaving the last job	116
Precocious kids one-up their teachers	117
Reasons to not mess with a child	118
The way children see things	119
Kids say the funniest things	120
Letter to a son in boot camp	122
Malapropisms	123
Big business mergers	124
Important things my mother taught me	125
The Norwegian perspective on life	126
Store open and closed sign confusion	127
Puzzling questions & things to ponder	128
The top 50 oxymorons	130
Where shall we all gather together?	131
Performance evaluations - actual quotes	131
How to drive in Phoenix, Arizona	132
The Pillsbury Doughboy Obituary	133
Disciplinary genius	133
Politically correct seasons greetings	134
Wise potato counsel	135
Sweet Revenge	135
Comparing prison and work	136
Phone out - Wake up - Think out of the box	137
International Pun Contest Winners	138
Frog seeks large bank loan	140
Once a pun a time	140
A few quarts low on the dipstick of life	141
Important Recall Notice	142
Letters of Recommendation	143
Retarded Grandparents	144
Which one way - Ski hospital - Last one way	145
S.A.T. Test Answers	146
Actual school excuse notes	147
Sensible advice and observations	149
Whatever comes to mind	150

Rejoice! Clean Humor

Smart answers	150
Brilliant crooks and criminal actions	151
As the memory begins to fade	152
What your computer is trying to tell you	153
To believe or not believe?	154
Keeping God out of public schools	155
A toast for friends and family	155
Did you know?	156
The most versatile two-letter word	157
Website name mistakes	158
Long sought answers to crucial questions	158
You have to try to laugh at all the taxes	159
Practical definitions	160
Dictionary for Women	160
It's great to be a man	161
CEO Power	161
Fascinating facts about the year 1904	162
Tell-tale signs of 21st century progress?	163
Insightful Wisdom	164
The sidewalk ends	165

✦✦✦ *And life's journey continues* ✦✦✦

170